I0698142

DEDICATION

"This book is a valuable resource crafted for independent podcasters who already have an established audience, much like myself, who aspire to navigate the intricate journey of successfully monetizing their podcasts. In its insightful pages, it unveils strategies, tips, and real-world examples that resonate with the unique challenges and aspirations of those who operate outside the traditional broadcasting landscape. Whether you're just starting or looking to elevate your podcasting game, this book provides a roadmap for understanding the intricacies of podcast monetization—from exploring diverse revenue streams to establishing authentic connections with advertisers. It's a comprehensive guide tailored to empower independent podcasters in turning their passion into a sustainable and thriving venture."

If you are just starting a podcast and in the process of building an audience please refer to my other book *"How To Become An Independent Podcaster Your Complete Guide"*.

How To Generate Income From Your Podcast

THE COMPLETE GUIDE

Jo Arcaya

INTRODUCTION

Podcasters achieve success through a dynamic combination of compelling content, audience engagement, and strategic monetization. At the heart of this success lies the ability to consistently deliver valuable and engaging content that resonates with the target audience. Building a loyal listener base involves fostering a sense of community through authentic communication and actively incorporating listener feedback. Successful podcasters are adept at adapting to the ever-evolving landscape of the podcasting industry, staying informed about emerging trends and technologies. Beyond content creation, strategic monetization plays a pivotal role. Diversifying revenue streams through sponsorships, affiliate marketing, listener donations, and premium content offerings ensures a sustainable income. Collaboration with other podcasters and leveraging social media platforms for promotion further amplifies the reach and impact of the podcast. Ultimately, the key to a podcaster's success lies in their passion for the subject matter, dedication to quality, and the ability to connect authentically with their audience.

CONTENTS

ACKNOWLEDGMENTS

In crafting the book "Make Money on Podcast," I am indebted to a multitude of individuals and resources that have contributed significantly to its creation. First and foremost, my heartfelt gratitude goes to the dedicated podcasters whose experiences and insights form the backbone of this guide. Their stories, challenges, and triumphs have enriched the narrative and provided valuable real-world perspectives.

I extend sincere appreciation to the podcasting community at large for fostering a collaborative environment and sharing knowledge that has shaped the content of this book. To the experts in the field who generously offered their expertise, thank you for illuminating the nuances of podcast monetization strategies.

I express profound thanks to my friends and family for their unwavering support, encouragement, and understanding during the writing process. Your belief in this project fueled my determination to create a resource that aspiring and seasoned podcasters alike can find valuable.

Finally, to the readers who embark on this journey to explore the world of podcast monetization, your curiosity and enthusiasm are the driving force behind the creation of "Make Money on Podcast." May this guide empower you with the knowledge and strategies needed to turn your passion for podcasting into a rewarding venture.

CHAPTER 1

Various Strategies

Monetizing a podcast involves various strategies to generate revenue from your content. I will be discussing every aspect of the following ways to monetize your podcast in each chapter. Here are some effective ways to monetize your podcast:

Sponsorships and Advertisements: Partner with relevant companies or brands for sponsorships and advertisements. Advertisers pay to promote their products or services during your podcast episodes.

Affiliate Marketing: Promote affiliate products or services within your podcast. Earn a commission for every sale made through your unique affiliate links.

Listener Donations: Encourage listener support through platforms like Patreon or Buy Me a Coffee. Offer exclusive content or perks to those who contribute.

Merchandising: Create and sell branded merchandise related to your podcast, such as T-shirts, mugs, or stickers. Platforms like Merch by Amazon can help you set up an online store.

Premium Content: Offer premium or exclusive content to subscribers who pay a monthly fee. This can include bonus episodes, early access, or behind-the-scenes content.

Crowdfunding: Launch crowdfunding campaigns on platforms like Kickstarter or Indiegogo to raise funds for your podcast. Offer rewards to backers based on their contribution level.

Live Events: Organize live podcast events or webinars and charge an admission fee. Engaging with your audience in real-time can create a unique and valuable experience.

Selling Courses or Workshops: If you have expertise in a specific area, create and sell online courses or workshops related to your podcast content.

Podcast Networks: Join podcast networks that connect you with advertisers and provide monetization opportunities. Some networks may offer revenue-sharing arrangements.

Subscription Models: Introduce a subscription model where listeners pay a fee to access ad-free episodes or additional content. Platforms like Apple Podcasts and Spotify are exploring subscription models.

License Your Content: License your podcast content to other platforms or media outlets for a fee. This can include syndication or partnerships with other media organizations.

Consulting Services: Offer consulting or coaching services based on your podcast expertise. Listeners who value your insights may be interested in one-on-one sessions.

Use Affiliate Codes: Incorporate affiliate codes in your podcast promotions. When listeners use these codes to make a purchase, you earn a commission.

Collaborate with Other Podcasters: Collaborate with other podcasters on joint ventures, sponsorships, or cross-promotions to expand your audience and revenue potential.

Choose a combination of these monetization strategies based on your podcast's niche, audience size, and content. Keep in mind that building a loyal and engaged audience is crucial for the success of your monetization efforts.

CHAPTER 2

Sponsorships and Advertisements

*I*n the realm of podcasting, Sponsorships and Advertisements emerge as integral components for creators seeking to transform their passion into a sustainable venture. These strategic partnerships not only provide financial support but also open doors to a broader audience and diverse opportunities. Sponsorships, marked by collaboration with brands or companies, allow podcasters to leverage their unique voice and content to endorse products or services. This symbiotic relationship enables creators to monetize their podcasts while introducing valuable offerings to their listeners. Simultaneously, strategically placed advertisements within episodes present a seamless way to diversify revenue streams.

This guide navigates the intricate landscape of securing sponsorships, negotiating deals, and seamlessly integrating advertisements into podcast content. Whether you're an experienced podcaster looking to enhance your monetization strategies or a newcomer eager to embark on a profitable journey, understanding the dynamics of Sponsorships and Advertisements is key to unlocking the full potential of your podcasting endeavors.

Securing sponsorships and advertising for podcasting involves a strategic approach and proactive efforts to attract brands or advertisers. Here's a step-by-step guide on how to get sponsorship and advertising for your podcast:

1. <u>Build a Strong and Niche Audience:</u> Focus on creating high-quality, niche-specific content that resonates with a dedicated audience. Brands are more likely to invest in podcasts with engaged listeners.

Building a strong and niche audience for your podcast is a deliberate and dynamic process that requires strategic planning and consistent effort. Begin by clearly defining your podcast's niche and target audience, understanding what sets your content apart. Craft compelling and relevant episodes that speak directly to the interests and needs of your audience, fostering a connection that goes beyond the surface. Leverage social media platforms, online communities, and other relevant channels to actively engage with your potential listeners. Create shareable content, tease upcoming episodes, and encourage audience participation through polls, Q&A sessions, or listener-submitted content. Consistency is key; establish a regular release schedule to build anticipation and reliability. Optimize your podcast for search engines by incorporating relevant keywords and creating eye-catching titles and descriptions. Encourage word-of-mouth marketing by prompting your existing audience to share your podcast with others who may share similar interests. Finally, seek feedback and adapt your content based on audience preferences, fostering a sense of community and loyalty. In doing so, you'll not only build a strong and engaged audience but also position your podcast for attracting potential sponsors and advertisers.

Let's say you're launching a podcast called "Artisan Eats Exposed," dedicated to exploring unique and niche culinary experiences. To build a strong and niche audience, focus on catering to food enthusiasts who appreciate rare, locally-sourced ingredients and unconventional cooking techniques. In each episode, delve into the world of artisanal food, featuring interviews with niche chefs, uncovering hidden food gems, and discussing the craftsmanship behind lesser-known culinary traditions. Your target audience might be individuals who see food as an art form and are passionate about discovering extraordinary gastronomic experiences.

To engage and grow this niche audience, utilize platforms like Instagram and Pinterest to share visually appealing content, such as behind-the-scenes glimpses of artisanal kitchens and visually stunning dishes. Join online communities or forums where food connoisseurs gather to discuss unique culinary finds. Encourage audience participation by inviting listeners to share their favorite artisanal food discoveries or submit questions for Q&A sessions with featured chefs.

By consistently delivering content that caters to the specific interests of this niche, you'll attract a dedicated community of food lovers who crave in-depth insights into the world of artisan eats. This approach not only builds a strong audience base but also positions your podcast as an authoritative voice within the niche, fostering a sense of community and enthusiasm among your listeners.

2. <u>Define Your Podcast Brand:</u> Clearly articulate your podcast's brand, values, and target audience. This information is crucial when approaching potential sponsors as it helps them understand the alignment between their brand and your content.

Defining your podcast brand is a crucial step in creating a distinct and memorable identity that resonates with your audience. Start by articulating the core theme and purpose of your podcast, identifying what sets it apart in a crowded digital landscape. Consider the tone and personality you want to convey—whether it's informative, conversational, humorous, or a unique blend that reflects your style. Establish a consistent visual identity through compelling artwork and a recognizable logo, ensuring that it aligns with the essence of your content. Clearly communicate your podcast's values and mission, emphasizing the benefits listeners can expect. Infuse your brand into every aspect of your podcast, from the content you produce to the way you engage with your audience on social media. Consistency in messaging, imagery, and overall presentation builds trust and fosters a stronger connection with your listeners, helping your podcast stand out and leave a lasting impression.

Let's imagine a podcast named "TechTrailblazers," dedicated to exploring the latest trends, innovations, and stories in the tech industry. To define the podcast brand, start with a compelling and consistent tagline like "Navigating the Future of Tech." This tagline succinctly communicates the podcast's mission to provide insights and guidance through the ever-evolving landscape of technology.

Next, establish a recognizable logo and visual identity that incorporates relevant tech elements, perhaps blending circuit patterns with a forward-looking arrow to symbolize progress. Choose a distinctive color scheme, such as a mix of vibrant blues and futuristic silvers, to create a visually appealing and cohesive brand image.

Craft a unique podcast intro that captures the essence of "TechTrailblazers," combining an engaging music score with a brief, energetic voiceover introducing the podcast's purpose and what listeners can expect.

Consistency is key across episodes. Develop a format that includes recurring segments, such as "Innovation Spotlight" or "Tech Trends Talk," to create a predictable yet dynamic structure. Maintain a consistent release schedule, whether it's weekly, bi-weekly, or monthly, to keep your audience engaged and anticipate new content regularly.

Finally, actively engage with your audience on social media platforms using the hashtag #TechTrailblazers to foster a sense of community. Respond to listener feedback, share behind-the-scenes glimpses, and leverage interactive elements like polls or Q&A sessions to strengthen the connection with your audience.

By defining a cohesive brand with a memorable tagline, visually appealing elements, a distinctive intro, consistent formatting, and active social media engagement, "TechTrailblazers" establishes itself as a trusted and recognizable source for navigating the exciting world of technology.

3. <u>Create a Professional Podcast:</u> Invest in good audio quality, engaging content, and a professional presentation. A polished podcast attracts both listeners and potential sponsors.

Creating a professional podcast involves a blend of technical finesse, engaging content, and thoughtful presentation. Begin by investing in quality audio equipment to ensure clear and crisp sound, mitigating any distractions for your listeners. Craft a compelling and structured format for your episodes, paying attention to pacing, transitions, and overall flow. Develop a consistent and recognizable podcast branding, including eye-catching cover art and a professional logo. Maintain a regular release schedule to establish reliability and keep your audience engaged. Edit your episodes meticulously, removing any unnecessary pauses, background noise, or disruptions to enhance the overall listening experience. Integrate captivating intros and outros to make a memorable impression. Additionally, consider incorporating music or sound effects judiciously to add flair without overshadowing your content. *Let's consider an example of creating a podcast called "CareerCraft Chronicles," focusing on career development tips and success stories.*

Define Your Niche and Audience: Clearly define the niche of your podcast, such as career development, and identify your target audience, which could be professionals, job seekers, or students.

Craft a Compelling Concept: Develop a unique and compelling concept for your podcast. For "CareerCraft Chronicles," the concept could revolve around sharing insights from successful professionals, offering career advice, and exploring industry trends.

Create a Professional Brand: Develop a professional brand for your podcast, including a distinctive logo, a memorable tagline like "Navigating Your Career Journey," and a consistent visual theme for promotional materials.

Invest in Quality Equipment: Acquire high-quality recording equipment, such as a microphone, headphones, and audio recording/editing software, to ensure clear and professional sound quality.

Plan Engaging Content: Plan your episodes with engaging and relevant content. This could include interviews with industry experts, success stories, Q&A sessions, and discussions on current job market trends.

Structure Your Episodes: Define a consistent episode structure. For "CareerCraft Chronicles," each episode could begin with a brief introduction, followed by the main content, and end with a call-to-action or teaser for the next episode.

Professional Hosting Platform: Choose a professional podcast hosting platform, such as Libsyn or Podbean, to host and distribute your episodes. Ensure your hosting service offers reliable analytics to track your podcast's performance.

Create Captivating Cover Art: Design eye-catching cover art that represents your podcast and attracts potential listeners. Use professional graphics and include relevant imagery related to career development.

Launch with Multiple Episodes: Launch your podcast with multiple episodes to give listeners a substantial introduction to your content. This also increases the chances of attracting and retaining subscribers.

Promote Effectively: Develop a comprehensive promotion strategy. Utilize social media platforms, create a dedicated website or blog, and collaborate with industry influencers to increase visibility.

Engage with Your Audience: Encourage listener interaction through social media, emails, or dedicated forums. Address listener questions, share behind-the-scenes content, and foster a sense of community.

Continuous Improvement: Regularly evaluate and improve your podcast based on listener feedback. Stay updated on industry trends and adapt your content accordingly.

By following these steps, "CareerCraft Chronicles" can establish itself as a professional and valuable resource for career development, attracting a dedicated audience and contributing to the success of its listeners' professional journeys.

4. <u>Understand Your Audience Analytics:</u> Use podcast analytics to gather data about your audience demographics, geographic location, and listener behavior. This information helps when pitching to sponsors who want to know about your reach.

Understanding your audience analytics is essential for tailoring your podcast content to meet the preferences and needs of your listeners. Utilize podcast hosting platforms that provide detailed analytics, including data on listener demographics, geographic locations, and listening devices. Analyze trends in episode downloads, listener retention, and audience growth to identify which topics or formats resonate most with your audience. Pay attention to listener feedback through comments, reviews, and social media interactions, as it offers valuable qualitative insights. Track the effectiveness of promotional efforts and marketing campaigns to understand what channels are most effective in reaching your target audience. Regularly reviewing and interpreting these analytics allows you to make data-driven decisions, refine your content strategy, and strengthen your connection with your audience over time. As you delve into the intricacies of your audience analytics, you gain valuable insights that empower you to deliver content that not only attracts but also retains and engages your listeners effectively.

Suppose you host a podcast called "Mindful Living Journey," focusing on personal development and mindfulness practices.

By leveraging podcast analytics, you can gain valuable insights into your audience. For example, through platforms like Apple Podcasts and Spotify, you discover that a significant portion of your listeners falls within the age range of 25 to 34. This data prompts you to tailor your content to align with the preferences and interests of this demographic, perhaps delving into topics like navigating career transitions and building mindful habits in a fast-paced world.

Geographically, analytics reveal a substantial listener base in urban areas, indicating a potential interest in topics related to mindfulness in busy city life. In response, you decide to feature episodes discussing mindfulness techniques for urban dwellers, managing stress in bustling environments, and fostering a mindful work-life balance.

Digging deeper into listener behavior, you find that episodes featuring guest interviews receive higher engagement. Armed with this knowledge, you decide to incorporate more guest interviews, reaching out to experts in various fields related to personal development and mindfulness.

By using podcast analytics to gather data about your audience's demographics, geographic location, and listener behavior, you not only understand your listeners better but also tailor your content to meet their specific needs and preferences. This strategic approach enhances audience engagement, attracts new listeners, and solidifies "Mindful Living Journey" as a podcast resonating with its target audience.

5. <u>Develop a Media Kit:</u> Create a comprehensive media kit that includes information about your podcast, audience demographics, download statistics, and sponsorship opportunities. Make it visually appealing and easy to understand.

Developing a media kit for your podcast is a strategic step to present a comprehensive and professional image to potential sponsors and collaborators. Start by outlining key information about your podcast, including its mission, target audience, and unique selling points. Incorporate compelling visuals such as your podcast logo, high-quality graphics, and any relevant images that showcase your brand. Provide essential statistics, such as download numbers, audience demographics, and listener engagement metrics, to demonstrate the reach and influence of your podcast. Clearly articulate the different sponsorship or advertising opportunities available, outlining the benefits sponsors can expect. Include testimonials, if available, to add credibility and showcase previous successful collaborations. Keep the media kit visually appealing, easy to navigate, and regularly update it to reflect your podcast's growth. A well-crafted media kit serves as a powerful tool to attract potential sponsors and establish fruitful partnerships by showcasing the unique value your podcast brings to the table.

For example, in the creation of a comprehensive media kit for a podcast named "BizInsights Unplugged," which focuses on business strategies and industry insights, various essential elements are included to attract potential sponsors. The media kit is designed to provide a clear overview of the podcast, its audience, download statistics, and available sponsorship opportunities.

Media Kit for BizInsights Unplugged:

Overview:

"BizInsights Unplugged is a dynamic and engaging podcast that dissects the latest trends, strategies, and success stories in the business world. Our in-depth interviews with industry leaders and expert analyses offer valuable insights for entrepreneurs, business professionals, and decision-makers."

<u>Audience Demographics:</u>

- *Age Range:* Primarily 25-54, with a significant presence in the 35-44 age group.

- *Geographic Location:* Strong listener base in major business hubs, including New York, San Francisco, and London.

- *Professions:* Diverse audience, ranging from small business owners to corporate executives, with a focus on industries such as tech, finance, and marketing.

<u>Download Statistics:</u>

- *Average Monthly Downloads:* 30,000+

- *Top-Performing Episodes:* Highlighting episodes with the highest engagement and listener retention.

- *Audience Growth:* Demonstrating consistent month-over-month growth in downloads.

<u>Sponsorship Opportunities:</u>

- *Title Sponsorship:* Exclusive mention in the podcast title and opening credits.

- *Segment Sponsorship:* Customized sponsorships for

specific segments or recurring features.

- *Episode Sponsorship:* Inclusion of sponsor messages within individual episodes.

- *Event Partnership:* Collaboration for live events or virtual summits related to business insights.

Why Sponsor BizInsights Unplugged?

- *Engaged and Targeted Audience:* Reach a highly engaged audience actively seeking business insights and strategies.

- *Visibility Across Platforms:* Exposure on major podcast platforms, our website, and social media channels.

- *Customizable Packages:* Tailored sponsorship packages to align with specific marketing goals and budgets.

Contact Information:

For inquiries and further details, please contact *[Your Name]* at *[Your Email Address]* or *[Your Phone Number]*.

This comprehensive media kit for "BizInsights Unplugged" serves as a valuable tool to showcase the podcast's appeal, audience demographics, strong download statistics, and the diverse range of sponsorship opportunities available for potential collaborators.

6. <u>Identify Potential Sponsors:</u> Research and identify brands or companies that align with your podcast's theme and audience. Consider both large and niche businesses that may find value in reaching your listeners.

Identifying potential sponsors for your podcast requires a strategic approach that aligns with your content and target audience. Begin by understanding your podcast's niche and audience demographics, as this knowledge will guide you in finding sponsors whose products or services resonate with your listeners. Research companies and brands that share a common interest or focus with your podcast's theme. Look for businesses that have a history of sponsoring podcasts or have a presence in your podcast's industry. Explore your personal network and industry connections for potential partnerships or recommendations. Utilize online platforms and directories designed to connect podcasters with potential sponsors. Tailor your pitch to emphasize the mutual benefits of collaboration, demonstrating how your podcast can provide value to the sponsor's target audience. By conducting thorough research and strategically aligning with brands that complement your content, you increase the likelihood of establishing meaningful and successful sponsorship relationships for your podcast.

Suppose you host a podcast called "Adventure Explorers," centered around travel, outdoor activities, and adventure experiences. Researching and identifying brands or companies that align with your podcast's theme and audience involves finding partnerships that resonate with adventure enthusiasts.

Here's an example:

Research and Partnership Identification for Adventure Explorers:

Podcast Theme Overview:

"Adventure Explorers is a thrilling podcast that dives into the world of exciting travel destinations, adrenaline-pumping outdoor activities, and inspiring adventure stories. Our audience comprises adventure seekers, outdoor enthusiasts, and travelers with a passion for exploring the unknown."

Identified Brands and Companies:

- *Outdoor Gear Brands:* Explore partnerships with renowned outdoor gear companies such as Patagonia, The North Face, or REI. Collaborate on episodes discussing essential gear, adventure travel packing tips, and product reviews.

- *Adventure Tour Operators:* Identify adventure travel companies like G Adventures or Intrepid Travel for potential partnerships. Feature episodes on unique adventure tours, destination highlights, and exclusive discounts for your listeners.

- *Travel Insurance Providers:* Partner with travel insurance companies that cater to adventure travelers. Discuss the importance of travel insurance in adventurous pursuits, share travel safety tips, and offer exclusive discounts for your audience.

- *Sustainable Travel Initiatives:* Collaborate with brands focused on sustainable and responsible travel, such as Earthwatch or Sustainable Travel International.

Showcase episodes on eco-friendly travel practices, conservation efforts, and eco-conscious adventure destinations.

- *Energy Snack Brands:* Connect with energy snack companies like Clif Bar or KIND Snacks. Feature episodes on nutrition tips for adventurers, discuss the best snacks for hiking or camping, and offer special promotions for your listeners.

<u>Approach Strategy:</u>

Craft personalized pitches for each identified brand, emphasizing the alignment between their values/products and the podcast's adventurous theme. Highlight the engaged and targeted audience of Adventure Explorers and how a partnership could provide valuable exposure to adventure enthusiasts.

<u>Why Partner with Adventure Explorers?</u>

- Access to a dedicated audience of adventure enthusiasts.

- Collaborative content that seamlessly integrates brands into the adventurous narrative.

- Cross-promotion through podcast episodes, social media, and the Adventure Explorers website.

This example demonstrates how to research and identify brands or companies that align with the podcast's theme and audience, fostering meaningful partnerships that enhance the listener experience and provide valuable exposure for the collaborating brands.

7. <u>Craft a Compelling Pitch:</u> Develop a personalized and compelling pitch for potential sponsors. Highlight the unique aspects of your podcast, the benefits of reaching your audience, and the value you can offer to the sponsor.

Crafting a compelling pitch for your podcast is a crucial step in attracting potential sponsors and advertisers. Begin by introducing your podcast with a concise and engaging overview, highlighting its unique value proposition and the specific audience it reaches. Clearly articulate the demographics and interests of your listeners, providing a detailed profile of why your podcast aligns with the sponsor's target market.

Next, emphasize the benefits of sponsoring your podcast, including the potential for increased brand exposure, engagement, and conversions. Showcase any relevant listener statistics, such as download numbers, audience demographics, and engagement metrics, to substantiate the reach and impact of your podcast.

Tailor your pitch to align with the sponsor's goals and values. Research the sponsor's brand, products, or services to demonstrate a genuine understanding of their business. Showcase how your podcast can authentically integrate their brand into the content, ensuring a seamless and meaningful connection with your audience.

Incorporate success stories or testimonials from previous sponsors, if available, to build credibility and illustrate the positive outcomes of partnering with your podcast. Be clear about the sponsorship opportunities available, whether it's through ad spots, sponsored segments, or other customized collaborations.

Crafting a compelling pitch requires a balance of creativity, data-driven insights, and a deep understanding of both your podcast and the potential sponsor's needs. By presenting a persuasive case that highlights the unique value and potential return on investment, you increase the likelihood of securing meaningful and successful partnerships for your podcast.

Let's consider a podcast named "Mindful Entrepreneur," which focuses on mindfulness practices, mental resilience, and personal growth tailored for entrepreneurs and business leaders. If you're reaching out to a potential sponsor, such as a wellness app or mindfulness training program, your pitch might look like this:

Subject: Exclusive Sponsorship Invitation: Elevate Mindfulness with Mindful Entrepreneur

Dear *[Sponsor's Name]*,

I hope this message finds you in good spirits. My name is *[Your Name]*, and I am the host of the transformative podcast, "Mindful Entrepreneur," where we explore the intersection of mindfulness and entrepreneurship, providing actionable insights for a balanced and resilient business journey.

About Mindful Entrepreneur:

Mindful Entrepreneur has quickly become a sanctuary for entrepreneurs seeking not only success in business but also a harmonious and mindful approach to their personal and professional lives.

Why [Sponsor's Name] is the Perfect Partner:

I've long admired *[Sponsor's Name]* for *[specific reasons, e.g., empowering individuals through mindfulness, commitment to mental well-being]*. Your organization's dedication to fostering mindfulness aligns seamlessly with the essence of "Mindful Entrepreneur."

Audience Demographics:

Our engaged audience comprises entrepreneurs, business leaders, and professionals seeking to integrate mindfulness into their hectic lives. With a strong presence in *[mention key demographics, e.g., 25-55 age group, business hubs]*, we have a direct reach to those actively shaping the entrepreneurial landscape.

What We Propose:

We envision a meaningful collaboration with *[Sponsor's Name]* that not only enhances your brand but also adds substantial value to our audience. Our proposed sponsorship package includes:

- *Mindfulness Workshops:* Feature your mindfulness experts in exclusive virtual workshops, providing practical techniques tailored for entrepreneurs.

- *Branding Excellence:* Elevate your brand through regular mentions in our episodes, ensuring a consistent presence in the hearts and minds of our mindful community.

- *Tailored Content Integration:* Work with us to create episodes that seamlessly integrate your brand's message, delivering authentic and actionable content.

Benefits of Partnership:

- *Targeted Entrepreneurial Community:* Connect with a focused audience passionate about mindful entrepreneurship and personal growth.

- *Authentic Integration:* Seamlessly integrate your brand into our content, ensuring an impactful and meaningful experience for our listeners.

- *Performance Analytics:* Gain insights into the impact of your sponsorship through detailed analytics and listener feedback.

Next Steps:

I am eager to discuss this exciting partnership opportunity further and explore how we can tailor it to align seamlessly with your brand's mission. Could we schedule a brief call at your earliest convenience?

Thank you for considering this opportunity to contribute to the mindful journey of entrepreneurs. I look forward to the prospect of collaborating with *[Sponsor's Name]*.

Warm regards,

[Your Full Name]

[Your Position]

[Your Contact Information]

This personalized pitch aims to communicate the unique value of "Mindful Entrepreneur," demonstrate alignment with the potential sponsor's brand, and outline the specific benefits of a partnership.

8. <u>Offer Sponsorship Packages:</u> Create different sponsorship packages that cater to various budgets. Include options for episode sponsorships, series sponsorships, or exclusive sponsorships, each with its own set of benefits.

Offering sponsorship packages for your podcast involves creating attractive and flexible options that cater to the varying needs and budgets of potential sponsors. Begin by developing a tiered system that provides different levels of exposure and benefits. For instance, create a basic package that includes standard ad placements, a mid-tier package with additional promotional opportunities, and a premium package offering exclusive features like sponsored segments, shout-outs, or extended coverage.

Clearly outline the specifics of each package, detailing the duration and frequency of ad placements, the platforms on which they will be featured, and any additional perks such as social media mentions or inclusion in newsletters. Consider incorporating various formats like pre-roll, mid-roll, or post-roll ads to cater to different preferences.

Highlight the unique advantages of each package and the potential reach and engagement sponsors can expect. Use data from your podcast analytics to showcase the size and demographics of your audience, emphasizing the value sponsors can derive from aligning with your content.

Ensure flexibility by allowing sponsors to customize packages based on their specific goals and preferences. Offer opportunities for sponsored content, interviews, or event collaborations to add an extra layer of uniqueness to the packages.

In your pitch, clearly communicate the call-to-action and the process for sponsors to secure their chosen package. Establish transparent communication channels, so sponsors feel confident about the partnership. By crafting well-defined, appealing sponsorship packages, you not only provide value to sponsors but also enhance the monetization potential of your podcast.

Let's create different sponsorship packages for a podcast named "Healthy Habits Hub," focusing on wellness, fitness, and healthy living. *These packages are designed to cater to various budgets and offer diverse options for potential sponsors.*

1. <u>Basic Wellness Booster Package:</u>
- *Episode Sponsorship (Standard):* Mention at the beginning and end of one episode.

- *Social Media Gratitude:* Recognition on our podcast's social media channels.

- *Logo Placement:* Featured on our website's sponsor

section.

2.   <u>Silver Wellness Enthusiast Package:</u>

- *Episode Sponsorship (Premium):* Inclusion in the opening and closing segments of two episodes per month.

- *Dedicated Social Media Post:* A personalized post showcasing your brand on our social media platforms.

- *Logo Placement with Link:* Prominent placement on our website with a clickable link.

- *30-second Wellness Tip:* A brief wellness tip or advice from your brand in one episode per month.

3.   <u>Gold Healthy Living Package:</u>

- *Series Sponsorship:* Your brand as the exclusive sponsor for a thematic series or set of episodes.

- *Bi-weekly Episode Inclusion:* Recognition in the opening and closing segments of every other episode.

- *Comprehensive Social Media Campaign:* A strategic and extended social media campaign featuring your brand.

- *Featured Blog Post:* An in-depth blog post on our website focusing on your brand and its connection to healthy living.

- *60-second Expert Spotlight:* An expert spotlight segment featuring your brand's insights in two episodes per month.

4.   <u>Platinum Lifestyle Wellness Package:</u>

- *Exclusive Sponsorship:* Be the exclusive sponsor for the entire podcast for a specified period.

- *Weekly Episode Inclusion:* Recognition in the opening and closing segments of every episode.

- *Premium Social Media Integration:* Customized and frequent social media engagement tailored to your brand's message.

- *Personalized Wellness Workshop:* A featured wellness workshop or session hosted by your brand.

- *Priority Logo Placement with Link:* Premium placement on our website with a clickable link.

- *90-second Lifestyle Insight:* A dedicated 90-second segment offering lifestyle insights from your brand in every episode.

These sponsorship packages are designed to accommodate various budgets while providing sponsors with a range of exposure and engagement options. They offer flexibility and customization to meet the specific goals and preferences of sponsors on "Healthy Habits Hub."

9. <u>Utilize Podcast Directories:</u> List your podcast in popular podcast directories and platforms that connect podcasters with potential sponsors, such as *Podchaser, Podcorn,* or *AdvertiseCast.*

Leveraging podcast directories is a strategic approach to increase the visibility and discoverability of your podcast. Start by ensuring your podcast is listed on popular directories like

Apple Podcasts, *Spotify*, *Google Podcasts*, and other platforms where users commonly search for and discover new content. Each directory has its submission process, which often involves providing essential information about your podcast, including its title, description, and category.

Optimize your podcast listing by crafting a compelling and concise description that accurately reflects the essence of your content. Use relevant keywords to enhance searchability and attract your target audience. Pay attention to cover art, ensuring it is eye-catching and aligns with your podcast's branding.

Encourage your audience to leave reviews and ratings on these platforms, as positive feedback can boost your podcast's ranking and attract more listeners. Engage with your audience through these directories, responding to comments and creating a sense of community around your podcast.

Podcast directories often offer additional features for podcasters, such as analytics and promotional opportunities. Familiarize yourself with these tools to track your podcast's performance and explore ways to increase its visibility.

Collaborate with other podcasters within these directories through cross-promotion or guest appearances, expanding your reach and attracting new listeners. Additionally, some directories connect podcasters with potential sponsors, providing opportunities for monetization.

Incorporating podcast directories into your overall podcast promotion strategy can significantly enhance your podcast's reach, making it more accessible to a broader audience and increasing the likelihood of attracting sponsors and advertisers.

10. <u>Network with Industry Contacts:</u> Attend industry events, conferences, or online forums related to podcasting and your podcast's niche. Networking can lead to potential sponsorship opportunities and collaborations.

Networking with industry contacts is a valuable strategy for growing your podcast and establishing meaningful connections within the podcasting community. Start by identifying key players in your podcast's niche or related industries. Attend industry events, conferences, or online webinars where you can engage with fellow podcasters, industry experts, and potential collaborators. Actively participate in discussions, ask questions, and share your insights to make a positive impression.

Utilize social media platforms to connect with industry contacts, join relevant groups, and participate in conversations. Platforms like Twitter, LinkedIn, and podcasting communities on platforms like Podchaser or Reddit can be excellent spaces to network and exchange ideas.

Consider reaching out to established podcasters for collaboration opportunities, whether through guest appearances on each other's shows or joint promotional efforts. Building relationships with influencers in your niche can amplify your podcast's reach and credibility.

Attend podcast meetups or organize your own local events to connect with podcasters in your area. Virtual networking can be just as effective, fostering connections with individuals from different geographical locations.

Be genuine in your interactions and seek to provide value to others in the industry. Share your expertise, promote other podcasts you enjoy, and offer support to fellow podcasters. Building a supportive network can lead to valuable insights, shared resources, and potential sponsorship opportunities.

Regularly engage with industry contacts, staying updated on trends and news. This not only enhances your knowledge but also positions you as an active and informed member of the podcasting community.

By actively networking with industry contacts, you not only expand your podcast's reach but also create a supportive ecosystem that can contribute to your podcast's growth, success, and potential for attracting sponsors and advertisers.

Let's explore an example scenario where a podcaster named Sarah attends a podcasting industry event called "PodConnect Expo," which focuses on diverse podcasting niches and brings together creators, industry professionals, and potential sponsors. *Here's how Sarah's experience at the event unfolds:*

PodConnect Expo: Unlocking Opportunities for the Podcast Pioneer

Sarah, host of the podcast "TechTrends Unleashed," eagerly attended this year's PodConnect Expo, an acclaimed podcasting industry event that promised a dynamic blend of networking, knowledge-sharing, and potential sponsorship opportunities. With a niche in technology and innovation, Sarah was on a mission to connect with like-minded individuals and explore collaborations that could elevate her podcast.

Upon arriving at the expo, Sarah immersed herself in

engaging panel discussions, gaining insights from industry experts on the latest podcasting trends, audience engagement strategies, and successful monetization models. During a session on podcast sponsorships, she learned about the importance of networking and building relationships within her niche.

Equipped with newfound knowledge, Sarah navigated the expo's bustling exhibition hall, where she encountered booths from tech companies, marketing agencies, and podcasting platforms. Here's how Sarah maximized her networking experience:

Connecting with Potential Sponsors:

Sarah engaged in meaningful conversations with representatives from tech companies whose products aligned with her podcast content. These interactions laid the foundation for potential sponsorship agreements, with discussions ranging from product integrations to dedicated segments on her show.

Niche Networking Events:

PodConnect Expo organized niche-specific networking events. Sarah attended the "Innovate & Elevate" mixer tailored for technology-focused creators. Here, she exchanged ideas, shared insights, and established connections with fellow podcasters, potential collaborators, and industry influencers.

Collaboration Discussions:

Sarah attended a collaborative content creation workshop, where she connected with content creators interested in cross-promotional opportunities. By discussing potential joint episodes and shared audience engagement strategies, Sarah laid the groundwork for collaborative ventures that could expand her podcast's reach.

Pitching Unique Sponsorship Opportunities:

Armed with a well-crafted pitch, Sarah approached potential sponsors with tailored sponsorship packages. She highlighted the unique value of "TechTrends Unleashed" and demonstrated how their brand could seamlessly integrate into her episodes, providing authentic value to her tech-savvy audience.

As a result of her proactive approach, Sarah not only expanded her network within the podcasting community but also secured preliminary discussions for potential sponsorships and collaborations. PodConnect Expo proved to be a pivotal platform, illustrating how strategic networking can unlock doors to exciting opportunities in the ever-evolving landscape of podcasting.

This example demonstrates how attending industry events can be a strategic move for podcasters seeking to enhance their network, explore collaboration possibilities, and open doors to potential sponsorship opportunities.

11. <u>Engage with Your Audience</u>: Foster a strong relationship with your audience through social media and other channels. Engaged listeners attract sponsors who want to tap into an active and responsive community.

Engaging with your audience is a fundamental aspect of building a strong and loyal community around your podcast. Start by establishing a presence on various social media platforms where your audience is likely to be active. Create dedicated profiles for your podcast and consistently share updates, behind-the-scenes content, and snippets from your episodes to keep your audience informed and intrigued.

Encourage audience participation by incorporating interactive elements into your podcast, such as Q&A segments, polls, or contests. Prompt your listeners to share their thoughts and opinions on social media or through podcast review platforms. Respond promptly to comments and messages, fostering a two-way conversation and making your audience feel valued.

Consider creating a dedicated space for your community, such as a Facebook group or Discord server, where listeners can connect with each other and discuss episodes. Actively participate in these communities to strengthen your connection with your audience.

Regularly seek and incorporate listener feedback into your content. This not only demonstrates that you value their opinions but also helps tailor your podcast to better meet their preferences.

Host live events, webinars, or virtual Q&A sessions where your audience can interact with you in real-time. These events provide a unique opportunity to deepen the connection with your listeners and gather insights into their interests.

Consistency is key in audience engagement. Stick to a regular posting schedule, and keep your audience informed about upcoming episodes, events, or any exciting developments related to your podcast.

By actively engaging with your audience, you not only create a sense of community but also cultivate a dedicated listener base that is more likely to share your content and attract potential sponsors interested in reaching an engaged and responsive audience.

Let's delve into an example of how a podcaster named Alex successfully fosters a strong relationship with their audience through social media, attracting sponsors eager to tap into an active and responsive community.

Building a Podcast Community: The Alex Audio Experience

Alex, the charismatic host of "The Alex Audio Experience," recognized the power of a strong and engaged community in attracting sponsors. With a podcast centered around personal development and life insights, Alex aimed to create not just a show but a vibrant community of listeners who actively participated in the podcast journey.

1. <u>Establishing a Presence on Social Media:</u>

Alex strategically utilized platforms like Instagram, Twitter, and a dedicated Facebook group to extend the podcast's reach. Consistent and authentic posts, engaging polls, and behind-the-scenes glimpses became the norm, creating an online space where listeners felt connected beyond the podcast episodes.

2. Fostering Two-Way Communication:

Instead of just broadcasting content, Alex encourages active participation. Regular Q&A sessions, listener-submitted topics, and shout-outs to engaged community members were incorporated into the podcast. This two-way communication made listeners feel valued and heard.

3. Exclusive Content and Sneak Peeks:

To reward loyal listeners, Alex shared exclusive content, bonus episodes, and sneak peeks into upcoming episodes on social media. This not only kept the audience excited but also created a sense of belonging for those actively engaging with the content.

4. Community Challenges and Events:

Alex organized community challenges related to personal development goals, encouraging listeners to share their progress. Live events, whether virtual or in-person meetups, provided an opportunity for the audience to connect with each other and with Alex, fostering a real sense of community.

5. Highlighting Listener Stories:

Regularly featuring listener stories and experiences on the podcast became a staple. This not only showcased the diverse perspectives within the community but also made listeners feel like an integral part of the podcast narrative.

Results: A Thriving Community Attracts Sponsors

As the community around "The Alex Audio Experience" flourished, sponsors took notice. They recognized the engaged and responsive nature of the audience, making it an attractive space for their brand to be featured. Sponsors were eager to align themselves with a podcast that not only had a substantial listener base but also boasted an actively involved community.

The relationship between Alex and the audience had transformed into a symbiotic partnership, where the podcast provided valuable content, and the audience, in turn, became brand advocates. This example illustrates how fostering a strong relationship with the audience through social media and other channels can create an environment that sponsors find irresistible—a community ready to engage with and support the brands that align with the podcast's values.

12. <u>Negotiate Fairly:</u> When negotiating sponsorship deals, be transparent and fair. Clearly outline deliverables, timelines, and any exclusivity agreements to ensure a mutually beneficial partnership.

Negotiating fairly for podcast sponsorships is a crucial skill that ensures both parties benefit from the collaboration. Begin by thoroughly understanding the value your podcast brings to sponsors, considering factors such as audience size, demographics, and engagement metrics. Armed with this information, establish a baseline for your sponsorship rates, taking into account industry standards and your podcast's unique strengths.

When entering negotiations, be transparent about your rates and the deliverables you can provide. Clearly articulate the benefits sponsors will receive, such as exposure to your audience, potential leads, or increased brand recognition. Emphasize the authenticity and engagement of your listeners, highlighting how their products or services align seamlessly with your content.

Consider offering different sponsorship packages to accommodate varying budgets and objectives. This flexibility allows sponsors to choose the level of exposure that best suits their needs while still ensuring fair compensation for your efforts.

Be open to discussion and willing to tailor sponsorship agreements to meet the specific goals of your sponsors. This collaborative approach fosters a positive relationship and increases the likelihood of long-term partnerships.

Understand the market value of your podcast and avoid undervaluing your content. At the same time, be realistic and flexible, especially when working with smaller businesses or startups. Negotiating fairly involves finding a balance that benefits both parties and sets the foundation for a successful and mutually rewarding partnership.

Regularly evaluate and adjust your sponsorship rates based on the growth of your podcast, increased audience size, and improvements in engagement metrics. Demonstrating the increasing value of your podcast over time justifies fair compensation and encourages sponsors to continue investing in your content.

By approaching sponsorship negotiations with transparency, flexibility, and a clear understanding of your podcast's worth, you contribute to building a sustainable and equitable podcasting ecosystem for both content creators and sponsors.

Let's explore an example of how a podcaster named Taylor negotiates a sponsorship deal with a tech company for their podcast, "Innovate Insights." Taylor prioritizes transparency and fairness to establish a mutually beneficial partnership:

Negotiating a Win-Win Sponsorship Deal: The Innovate Insights Podcast

Taylor, the host of the "Innovate Insights" podcast focusing on technology trends and innovations, was approached by a prominent tech company, InnovateTech Solutions, for a potential sponsorship deal. Recognizing the importance of transparency and fairness in negotiations, Taylor took a strategic approach to outline clear terms that would benefit both parties.

1. <u>Initial Meeting</u>:

Taylor initiated an initial meeting with representatives from InnovateTech Solutions to understand their marketing goals, target audience, and expectations from the sponsorship. This laid the foundation for a collaborative discussion centered around shared objectives.

2. Transparent Audience Insights:

Taylor provided detailed audience demographics and insights, showcasing the podcast's reach, listener engagement, and alignment with tech enthusiasts. Transparency about the podcast's performance allowed InnovateTech Solutions to make an informed decision.

3. Customized Sponsorship Packages:

Recognizing that one size doesn't fit all, Taylor proposed different sponsorship packages tailored to meet InnovateTech Solutions' marketing objectives. Each package included specific deliverables, such as sponsored episodes, mentions, and social media promotions.

4. Clearly Defined Deliverables:

In the negotiation process, Taylor clearly outlined what each sponsorship package entailed. This included the number of sponsored episodes, the frequency of mentions, and the duration of social media promotions. By specifying deliverables, both parties had a transparent understanding of expectations.

5. Timelines and Schedule:

Taylor proposed a well-defined timeline for the sponsorship activation, specifying when sponsored episodes would air, social media promotions would take place, and any additional promotional events would occur. This ensured that both parties were on the same page regarding the schedule.

6. <u>Exclusivity Agreements:</u>

If applicable, Taylor discussed any exclusivity agreements to prevent conflicts with competitors. By being transparent about exclusivity terms, Taylor demonstrated a commitment to preserving the integrity of the sponsorship for InnovateTech Solutions.

7. <u>Mutually Agreed Terms:</u>

Through open and honest discussions, Taylor and InnovateTech Solutions negotiated terms that were agreeable to both parties. Any adjustments to the proposed sponsorship packages were made collaboratively, fostering a sense of partnership.

Results: A Mutually Beneficial Partnership

The negotiation process between Taylor and InnovateTech Solutions resulted in a mutually beneficial partnership. The podcast gained a reputable sponsor aligned with its niche, and InnovateTech Solutions gained exposure to a highly engaged audience. The transparent and fair approach to negotiations laid the groundwork for a successful, long-term collaboration between "Innovate Insights" and InnovateTech Solutions.

This example illustrates the importance of transparency and fairness in negotiating sponsorship deals, ensuring that both the podcaster and the sponsor are well-informed and satisfied with the terms of the partnership.

13. <u>Measure and Showcase Results:</u> Track the performance of sponsored content and regularly share analytics with sponsors. Demonstrating the impact of their investment increases the likelihood of continued partnerships.

Measuring and showcasing results for your podcast is essential to demonstrate the value you provide to sponsors and to attract future collaborations. Begin by leveraging podcast analytics tools to gather data on key performance indicators (KPIs) such as download numbers, listener demographics, and listener retention rates. These metrics offer insights into the reach and engagement of your podcast.

Highlight specific episodes or campaigns that performed exceptionally well, showcasing their impact on audience growth and engagement. Identify trends in listener behavior to understand which content resonates the most with your audience.

Incorporate listener feedback and testimonials into your results showcase. Positive reviews and comments not only provide qualitative insights into the impact of your podcast but also serve as social proof of its value.

Create visually appealing reports or infographics that encapsulate your podcast's success story. Graphs, charts, and statistics can effectively communicate growth trends and milestones to sponsors in a digestible format.

Regularly update your media kit with the latest results and achievements, ensuring that sponsors have access to the most recent and compelling data when considering partnerships. This transparency and proactivity in sharing results build trust and credibility with sponsors.

When showcasing results to sponsors, emphasize the tangible benefits they have gained from the collaboration. This could include increased brand visibility, website traffic, or engagement with their products or services. Clearly communicate the return on investment (ROI) they achieved by partnering with your podcast.

Consider hosting virtual meetings or webinars to personally present your podcast's results to sponsors. This allows for a direct and interactive discussion where you can address any questions, provide additional context, and strengthen the relationship with your sponsors.

Ultimately, the ability to measure and effectively showcase results is not only a testament to your podcast's success but also a powerful tool for attracting sponsors who seek a measurable impact from their investments.

Remember, the process of securing sponsorships takes time, persistence, and a genuine commitment to creating valuable content. As your podcast grows and gains recognition, attracting sponsors becomes increasingly achievable.

Let's explore an example of how a podcaster named Jordan tracks the performance of sponsored content for the podcast "Wellness Waves" and regularly shares analytics with a health and fitness brand, FitLife Boost, to demonstrate the impact of their investment:

Optimizing Impact: Analytics-Driven Sponsored Content on Wellness Waves

Jordan, the host of the "Wellness Waves" podcast, prioritizes transparency and effectiveness when it comes to sponsored content. FitLife Boost, a health and fitness brand, had recently sponsored a series of episodes. To ensure the brand recognized the impact of their investment, Jordan implemented a robust analytics tracking and reporting strategy.

1. Detailed Analytics Integration:

Jordan utilized podcast analytics tools to track key performance indicators, including listener demographics, download statistics, and engagement metrics. These insights provided a comprehensive understanding of how FitLife Boost's sponsored content resonated with the audience.

2. Episode-Specific Metrics:

Recognizing the importance of granularity, Jordan tracked metrics specific to the sponsored episodes. This included listener retention rates during sponsored segments, click-through rates on unique promotional links, and social media engagement related to the sponsored content.

3. Regularly Scheduled Reports:

Jordan established a routine for generating and sharing analytics reports with FitLife Boost. Monthly reports were comprehensive, outlining performance trends, audience growth, and the specific impact of FitLife Boost's sponsorship on the podcast's overall metrics.

4. Impactful Visualizations:

To enhance clarity, Jordan presented data through visually appealing graphs and charts. These visualizations highlighted key performance indicators, showcasing trends and demonstrating the correlation between sponsored content and audience engagement.

5. Customized Insights:

Jordan went beyond raw data by providing customized insights into listener feedback, comments, and interactions related to FitLife Boost's sponsored content. This qualitative information added depth to the quantitative metrics, offering a holistic view of the sponsorship's impact.

6. Goal Achievement Highlights:

If FitLife Boost had specific goals or key performance indicators they wanted to achieve through the sponsorship, Jordan highlighted instances where those goals were met or exceeded. Celebrating achievements reinforced the positive impact of the partnership.

7. Proactive Communication:

Jordan maintained open communication with FitLife Boost, not only during the reporting periods but also whenever noteworthy developments occurred. Whether it was a spike in downloads, positive social media mentions, or relevant industry recognition, Jordan kept FitLife Boost informed.

Results: Long-Term Partnership and Renewed Commitment

By consistently tracking and sharing detailed analytics, Jordan demonstrated the tangible impact of FitLife Boost's sponsorship on "Wellness Waves." FitLife Boost, impressed by the transparency and measurable results, not only extended their initial sponsorship commitment but also increased their investment in subsequent campaigns. The data-driven approach not only solidified FitLife Boost's confidence in the partnership but also paved the way for a long-term collaboration based on mutual success.

This example highlights the importance of using analytics to track sponsored content performance and the positive impact of transparent reporting in fostering long-term partnerships with sponsors.

CHAPTER 3

Affiliate Marketing

Promote affiliate products or services within your podcast. Earn a commission for every sale made through your unique affiliate links.

Promoting affiliate products on your podcast can be a lucrative way to monetize your content. Here are some strategies to effectively promote affiliate products:

1. <u>Choose Relevant Products:</u> Select affiliate products that align with your podcast's niche and audience interests. Products that genuinely resonate with your audience are more likely to result in successful conversions.

Let's explore an example of how a podcaster named Jamie strategically selects affiliate products that align with the podcast's niche and audience interests, leading to successful conversions.

Podcast: Culinary Connoisseur Chronicles

Jamie, the host of the "Culinary Connoisseur Chronicles" podcast, has cultivated a dedicated audience of food enthusiasts and home cooks. Recognizing the potential of affiliate marketing to monetize the podcast, Jamie decides to carefully curate affiliate products that resonate with the podcast's niche and the interests of the audience.

1. Researching Audience Preferences:

Jamie conducts surveys, engages with listeners on social media, and analyzes podcast analytics to understand the specific interests and preferences of the audience. This reveals that many listeners are passionate about gourmet cooking, kitchen gadgets, and unique ingredients.

2. Partnering with Gourmet Ingredient Brands:

Armed with insights, Jamie seeks affiliate partnerships with gourmet ingredient brands that offer high-quality, unique products. These could include specialty spices, rare cooking oils, or artisanal chocolates. Aligning with these brands ensures that the products are not only relevant but also exciting for the audience.

3. Featuring Cooking Gadgets and Tools:

Understanding that the audience is also interested in enhancing their culinary skills, Jamie explores affiliations with companies that offer innovative cooking gadgets and tools. This could range from high-quality knives to smart kitchen appliances. Each affiliate product is selected based on its utility and appeal to the podcast's culinary-focused audience.

4. <u>Incorporating Affiliate Products Naturally:</u>

Instead of delivering generic ad-reads, Jamie seamlessly incorporates affiliate products into the podcast content. For example, during an episode discussing chocolate-based desserts, Jamie introduces a unique artisanal chocolate brand as an affiliate, explaining how it can elevate the audience's dessert creations.

5. <u>Sharing Personal Experiences:</u>

Jamie doesn't just present affiliate products as advertisements but shares personal experiences and recommendations. This authentic approach builds trust with the audience, making them more inclined to consider and trust the recommended products.

6. <u>Exclusive Discounts and Promotions:</u>

Negotiating exclusive discounts or promotions with affiliate partners, Jamie sweetens the deal for the audience. This not only adds value for listeners but also serves as an incentive for them to make a purchase, benefiting both the audience and the affiliate brands.

7. <u>Monitoring Conversions and Feedback:</u>

Using tracking links and analytics, Jamie monitors the performance of affiliate products. Regularly reviewing conversion rates and listener feedback helps fine-tune the selection process and ensures that future affiliate partnerships align even more closely with the audience's preferences.

Results: Successful Conversions and Satisfied Audience:

By meticulously selecting affiliate products that align with the podcast's niche and audience interests, Jamie sees an increase in successful conversions. The audience appreciates the curated recommendations, and the podcast monetizes effectively without compromising the listener experience. The authenticity in product selection and presentation fosters a positive relationship between "Culinary Connoisseur Chronicles" and its audience.

This example illustrates how thoughtful selection of affiliate products, aligned with the podcast's niche and audience interests, can lead to successful conversions and a satisfied listener base.

2. <u>Integrate Naturally into Content:</u> Incorporate affiliate product mentions organically into your podcast content. Avoid sounding too promotional; instead, seamlessly integrate the product into relevant discussions or recommend it as a solution to a problem.

Incorporating affiliate product mentions organically into your podcast content is essential to ensure that promotions seamlessly fit within the narrative and resonate with your audience. Begin by identifying natural touch points within your episodes where product mentions would make sense. These could be moments related to problem-solving, personal anecdotes, or discussions about industry trends. Rather than forcing a promotional message, integrate the product recommendation authentically into the conversation, ensuring it enhances the overall content.

Craft a compelling story or scenario around the affiliate product to make it more relatable to your audience. Share personal experiences or insights about how the product has positively impacted your life, making the endorsement more authentic and trustworthy. Avoid sounding overly promotional or scripted; instead, maintain a conversational tone that aligns with your usual podcast style.

Consider creating dedicated segments or episodes focused on reviewing or discussing affiliate products in-depth. This provides a dedicated space for thorough exploration while giving your audience valuable insights into the features and benefits of the recommended products.

Utilize visual elements on your podcast's website or social media platforms to complement your audio content. Incorporate engaging graphics, images, or short video clips that showcase the affiliate product, creating a multimedia experience for your audience.

Offer exclusive promotions, discounts, or bonuses tied to the affiliate products, making the mentions more enticing for your listeners. Clearly communicate these exclusive offers during your podcast, emphasizing the added value they bring to your audience.

By seamlessly integrating affiliate product mentions into your podcast content, you enhance the overall listening experience for your audience. This approach ensures that promotions feel natural, valuable, and genuinely aligned with your podcast's theme, fostering trust and increasing the likelihood of listener engagement and conversions.

Let's explore an example of how a podcaster named Emma incorporates affiliate product mentions organically into her podcast conte

nt, ensuring a seamless integration without sounding overly promotional.

Podcast: Wellness Whispers with Emma

Emma, the host of "Wellness Whispers," a podcast centered around holistic health and self-care, understands the importance of maintaining an authentic and non-intrusive approach when incorporating affiliate product mentions. She aims to seamlessly integrate relevant products into her content to enhance the listener experience.

1. Episode Topic: Stress Relief Techniques

In an episode focusing on stress relief techniques, Emma identifies an opportunity to introduce an affiliate product that aligns with the theme.

2. Natural Progression in the Conversation:

Emma starts by discussing various stress management methods, including meditation, aromatherapy, and relaxation techniques. As the conversation naturally progresses, she introduces the affiliate product – a premium aromatherapy essential oil diffuser.

3. Storytelling Approach:

Rather than presenting the diffuser as a standalone promotional item, Emma weaves it into a personal anecdote. She shares a story about how incorporating aromatherapy into her daily routine significantly reduced her stress levels.

4. Recommending a Solution:

Emma seamlessly recommends the affiliate product as a potential solution to her listeners. She emphasizes its positive impact on creating a calming atmosphere, enhancing relaxation, and fostering a sense of well-being.

5. Highlighting Features and Benefits:

While discussing the diffuser, Emma subtly highlights its features and benefits without sounding like a commercial. She focuses on how it offers adjustable settings, uses high-quality essential oils, and complements various wellness practices.

6. Exclusive Offer for Listeners:

Emma sweetens the deal for her audience by negotiating an exclusive offer or discount for listeners who use a specific code when purchasing the affiliate product. This adds value for her audience and provides an extra incentive for them to consider the recommendation.

7. <u>Open Invitation for Feedback</u>:

Emma encourages listener engagement by inviting feedback and experiences related to the recommended product. This not only fosters a sense of community but also allows her to gauge the audience's response and adjust future affiliate integrations accordingly.

Results: Enhanced Listener Experience and Organic Engagement:

By incorporating the affiliate product mentioned organically into the content, Emma successfully avoids a promotional tone. Her listeners appreciate the genuine recommendation seamlessly woven into the episode, contributing to an enhanced overall listener experience. The affiliate product integrates seamlessly into the conversation, aligning with the podcast's theme and providing value to the audience without disrupting the natural flow of the content.

This example demonstrates how a podcaster can organically incorporate affiliate product mentions into their content, maintaining authenticity and relevance while avoiding a promotional tone.

3. <u>Create Dedicated Segments or Episodes:</u> Devote specific segments or episodes to reviewing or discussing affiliate products in-depth. This allows you to provide valuable insights, share personal experiences, and educate your audience about the benefits of the products.

Here's a guide on how to create dedicated segments or episodes:

<u>Define the Purpose of the Segment</u>: Clearly define the purpose of the dedicated segment or episode. Whether it's a Q&A session, a guest interview, or a product review, having a clear objective helps structure the content and provides a focused experience for your audience.

<u>Choose Relevant Topics</u>: Select topics that align with your podcast's theme and cater to your audience's interests. For affiliate promotions, choose topics that naturally integrate with the products you'll be endorsing. Relevance is key to maintaining audience engagement.

Example in curating content for a wellness and lifestyle blog, selecting relevant topics that resonate with the target audience is paramount. Let's imagine the blog caters to a health-conscious readership interested in holistic well-being. In this context, relevant topics could include articles on mindful living, balanced nutrition, and mental health. For instance, one could explore "The Benefits of Mindful Meditation for Stress Reduction" to address the growing interest in mental wellness.

Additionally, topics like "Incorporating Superfoods into Your Daily Diet" align with the audience's focus on nutrition. By delving into subjects that directly align with the readers' interests and aspirations, such as maintaining a balanced lifestyle and nurturing both mental and physical health, the blog can effectively engage its audience and establish itself as a go-to resource for holistic well-being.

Establish a Consistent Format: Establish a consistent format for your dedicated segments. This could include a specific introduction, a defined structure for discussing key points, and a conclusion. Consistency creates a sense of familiarity for your listeners.

When creating a podcast, ensuring a consistent and recognizable format for dedicated segments is vital for audience engagement and brand identity. Let's consider a podcast focused on personal development and career growth. To establish a consistent format, the show could introduce a recurring segment named "Career Insights Wednesdays." Each Wednesday episode might feature interviews with successful professionals, sharing their career journeys, challenges, and advice for listeners. Another segment, perhaps called "Monday Motivation Minute," could kick off the week with a brief inspirational message or a quick tip to boost motivation. By maintaining a regular schedule and thematic consistency with these dedicated segments, listeners can anticipate and look forward to specific content on particular days. This not only provides a structured listening experience but also reinforces the podcast's identity, making it more memorable and appealing to a broader audience interested in personal and professional development.

Announce and Introduce the Segment: Clearly announce and introduce the dedicated segment at the beginning of your podcast episode. Set expectations for your audience, informing them about the upcoming focus and explaining how it adds value to their listening experience.

Imagine launching a podcast focused on exploring intriguing historical mysteries. To ensure a structured and engaging listening experience, it's essential to clearly announce and introduce dedicated segments at the beginning of each episode. You could begin with a distinctive jingle or a brief musical intro to signal the start of the show. Following this, you might have a segment called "Mystery Spotlight," where each episode delves into a different historical enigma. To introduce this segment, the host could use a scripted opening, saying something like, "Welcome to another episode of 'Unsolved Histories.' I'm your host, [Host Name], and today we kick off with our signature segment, 'Mystery Spotlight.' Get ready to journey through time as we unravel a fascinating historical puzzle that has puzzled historians for centuries." By clearly announcing and introducing the dedicated segment right from the start, listeners are instantly oriented, creating anticipation and setting the tone for the episode ahead. This approach contributes to a cohesive and engaging podcast experience.

Feature Guest Collaborations: Consider featuring guest collaborations within your dedicated segments. Invite experts, industry professionals, or individuals with unique perspectives related to the segment's theme. Guest collaborations add diversity and depth to your content.

In optimizing the content strategy for a podcast focused on technology trends, an effective approach could involve featuring guest collaborations within dedicated segments. For instance, imagine a segment named "Innovator Interviews," where each episode showcases conversations with leading figures in the tech industry. To introduce this collaborative element, the host could begin the episode by saying, "Welcome to another episode of 'TechTalk Unleashed.' Today, we have a special treat for you in our 'Innovator Interviews' segment. Joining us is [Guest Name], a trailblazer in [specific tech domain], here to share insights, experiences, and predictions on the latest technological advancements." Integrating guest collaborations not only injects fresh perspectives but also brings in varied expertise, enriching the content and offering listeners diverse insights. This strategy fosters audience engagement and establishes the podcast as a dynamic platform for thought leadership within the tech community.

Promote Affiliate Products Naturally: Integrate affiliate product mentions naturally within the dedicated segment. For instance, if the episode focuses on productivity, seamlessly introduce and discuss relevant affiliate tools or resources that can enhance productivity for your audience.

Suppose you're hosting a podcast centered around health and wellness, and you have a dedicated segment called "Wellness Picks Wednesday," where you discuss and recommend various products contributing to a healthy lifestyle. To seamlessly integrate affiliate product mentions within this segment, you could start by introducing the segment with an engaging hook: "Hello, health enthusiasts! Welcome to another 'Wellness Picks Wednesday,' the segment where we explore top-notch products that can elevate your well-being. Today, I'm excited to share a personal favorite of mine – *[Affiliate Product]*. I've been using it for *[specific benefit]*, and it's truly made a positive impact on my daily routine." Following this introduction, delve into a genuine and informative discussion about the affiliate product, highlighting its features, benefits, and how it aligns with the theme of the podcast. By integrating these mentions organically and sincerely, you provide valuable recommendations to your audience while also creating a potential revenue stream through affiliate partnerships. This approach ensures that the product mentions feel authentic and contribute to the overall value of the dedicated segment.

Maintain a Conversational Tone: Keep the tone of your dedicated segments conversational and engaging. Avoid sounding overly scripted or promotional. A natural and authentic approach resonates better with listeners and contributes to a positive listening experience.

Encourage Audience Interaction: Actively encourage audience interaction within dedicated segments. Invite listeners to share their thoughts, ask questions, or participate in discussions related to the segment's theme. This interaction fosters a sense of community and engagement.

Utilize Multimedia Elements: Enhance the dedicated segments by incorporating multimedia elements. This could include visuals, such as charts, images, or short video clips, on your podcast's website or social media platforms. Multimedia elements complement the audio content and provide a more comprehensive experience.

Follow Up and Recap: Consider following up on dedicated segments in subsequent episodes. Provide recaps, share listener feedback, and offer additional insights or updates related to the discussed topics. This ongoing engagement keeps your content dynamic and encourages continued interest.

Promote Exclusive Offers: Tie dedicated segments to exclusive offers or promotions related to affiliate products. Creating special deals or discounts exclusively for your audience enhances the value proposition and incentivizes listeners to explore the endorsed products.

This approach not only adds variety to your episodes but also allows you to deliver targeted and valuable content to your audience while integrating affiliate marketing in an authentic manner.

4. <u>Offer Exclusive Discounts or Promotions:</u> Negotiate with the affiliate partners to provide exclusive discounts or promotions for your podcast audience. Unique incentives encourage listeners to use your affiliate links and enhance the value proposition.

Offering exclusive discounts or promotions on your podcast is an excellent way to incentivize your audience to engage with affiliate products.

Here are a few examples of how you can effectively provide exclusive offers:

Coupon Codes for Listeners: Negotiate with your affiliate partners to secure unique coupon codes for your podcast listeners. During the episode, share these exclusive codes, explaining that they provide special discounts or additional benefits. This not only adds value for your audience but also tracks the effectiveness of your promotions.

Limited-Time Offers: Create a sense of urgency by promoting limited-time offers tied to specific episodes.

Encourage your listeners to take advantage of exclusive discounts or promotions within a short timeframe, creating a compelling reason for them to act promptly.

Bundle Deals for Listeners: Arrange with affiliate partners to create exclusive bundle deals or package offers specifically for your podcast audience. Highlight the added value of these bundles during your episodes, emphasizing that they are available only to your listeners for a limited period.

Free Trials with Promo Codes: If the affiliate product offers a free trial, collaborate with the partner to provide listeners with special promo codes for extended or enhanced trial periods. This allows your audience to experience the product more comprehensively before making a purchasing decision.

Access to Premium Content: Partner with affiliates who offer premium or exclusive content. Negotiate special access for your listeners, whether it's exclusive guides, webinars, or additional resources. Promote these perks as part of the affiliate product package, creating added value for your audience.

Contests and Giveaways: Combine the excitement of contests or giveaways with affiliate promotions. Encourage listeners to participate for a chance to win exclusive prizes or products from your affiliates. This not only boosts engagement but also generates interest in the promoted products.

Affiliate-Branded Merchandise: Collaborate with affiliates to create exclusive, co-branded merchandise for your podcast. Offer these items as part of a promotion, providing listeners with a unique opportunity to receive special merchandise alongside their affiliate product purchase.

VIP Access or Early Releases: Secure VIP access or early release privileges for your audience with certain affiliate products. Highlight these perks during your podcast episodes, emphasizing that your listeners have the exclusive advantage of being among the first to access new features or updates.

Stackable Discounts for Listeners: Work with affiliates to offer stackable discounts for your audience. This means combining various discounts or promotions to provide a more substantial overall offer. Clearly communicate the stackable nature of these benefits during your podcast episodes.

Specialized Support or Training Sessions: Collaborate with affiliates to provide specialized support or training sessions for your listeners. Whether it's a dedicated customer support line or exclusive training webinars, these additional services can be promoted as exclusive benefits for your audience.

When promoting these exclusive offers, emphasize their limited availability and the unique advantages they bring to your listeners. Creating a sense of exclusivity and additional value enhances the appeal of affiliate products and encourages your audience to take action.

5. <u>Disclose Affiliation Transparently:</u> Maintain transparency with your audience by clearly disclosing your affiliation with the promoted products. Honest and transparent communication fosters trust and credibility with your listeners.

Maintaining transparency with your audience is crucial when incorporating affiliate promotions into your podcast. Clearly disclosing your affiliation with promoted products builds trust and ensures openness.

Here's how to do it effectively:

> *<u>Introduction and Acknowledgment</u>:* Begin the segment or episode by transparently acknowledging your affiliation with the products you are about to discuss. A straightforward introduction sets the tone for openness, and it shows your audience that you value their trust.
>
> *<u>Explain the Affiliate Relationship</u>:* Take a moment to explain what an affiliate relationship entails. Briefly describe that you may earn a commission if your audience decides to make a purchase using the provided affiliate links. This educates your listeners about the nature of the partnership.
>
> *<u>Highlight the Benefits for Your Audience</u>:* Emphasize how the affiliate partnerships benefit your audience. Clarify that

these relationships enable you to continue creating valuable content and maintain the quality of your podcast without relying solely on traditional advertising methods.

Share Personal Criteria for Endorsements: Communicate the criteria you use when selecting products to endorse. Assure your audience that you only promote products that align with your values, meet high-quality standards, and genuinely provide value to them. This transparency helps build credibility.

Disclose Early and Clearly: Disclose your affiliation early in the episode or segment, preferably before delving into the details of the affiliate products. Being upfront ensures that your audience is aware of your relationship from the outset, promoting a sense of honesty and openness.

Repeat Disclosures Periodically: Reiterate your disclosure periodically, especially if the affiliate promotions are spread across multiple segments or episodes. Remind your audience about your affiliations as a form of reinforcement, ensuring that the information is consistently communicated.

Use Clear Language: Employ clear and straightforward language when disclosing your affiliation. Avoid jargon or convoluted explanations. Your audience should easily understand the nature of your relationship with the promoted products and how it may impact your content.

Provide Contact Information for Questions: Invite your audience to reach out if they have any questions or concerns about your affiliations. Providing contact information, such as an email address or social media handles, encourages open communication and demonstrates your commitment to transparency.

Separate Editorial Content from Promotions: Clearly distinguish between regular editorial content and promotional segments. Whether through distinct introductions, background music, or other audio cues, creating separation helps your audience identify when you are discussing affiliate products.

Educate Your Audience About Affiliate Marketing: Dedicate a brief moment to educate your audience about the affiliate marketing model. Explain that it is a common practice in the digital space and that it doesn't affect the integrity of your reviews or recommendations.

Act on Audience Feedback: Actively listen to audience feedback and address any concerns related to transparency. If your listeners express uncertainties or request additional information, use that feedback to refine your disclosure practices and maintain a transparent relationship.

By consistently and transparently disclosing your affiliations with promoted products, you foster a trusting relationship with your audience. Open communication about your partnerships demonstrates your commitment to honesty and integrity, reinforcing the credibility of your podcast content.

6. Create Engaging Call-to-Actions: Craft compelling calls-to-action (CTAs) that encourage listeners to take immediate action, such as visiting an affiliate link or using a special promo code. Create a sense of urgency to drive conversions.

Crafting compelling calls-to-action (CTAs) in your podcast is essential to motivate listeners to take immediate action.

Here's a guide on how to create CTAs that effectively encourage engagement:

> *Be Clear and Concise:* Start by being clear and concise in your CTAs. Clearly state what action you want your listeners to take and why it's beneficial for them. Avoid ambiguity to ensure your message resonates clearly.

> *Create a Sense of Urgency:* Infuse urgency into your CTAs to prompt immediate action. Use phrases like "limited time offer," "act now," or "exclusive for the next 24 hours" to create a sense of urgency and encourage listeners to take action promptly.

> *Highlight Benefits:* Emphasize the benefits of the action you're asking listeners to take. Clearly articulate how engaging in the suggested activity will add value to their

lives, whether it's saving money, gaining exclusive access, or improving their overall experience.

Use Persuasive Language: Employ persuasive language that resonates with your audience. Appeal to their emotions and needs, making them feel compelled to respond. Use words that evoke a sense of excitement, curiosity, or satisfaction.

Make it Easy to Follow: Ensure that your CTA is easy to follow. Clearly outline the steps your audience needs to take, whether it's visiting a website, using a promo code, or subscribing to a newsletter. Simplifying the process increases the likelihood of listener engagement.

Incorporate a Strong Verbal Delivery: Your verbal delivery is crucial in conveying the urgency and importance of your CTA. Use a confident and enthusiastic tone to convey excitement and conviction. Maintain a conversational style to connect with your audience on a personal level.

Provide Multiple Engagement Options: Offer various channels or platforms through which listeners can engage. Whether it's visiting a website, following on social media, or subscribing to a newsletter, providing multiple options accommodates diverse preferences and increases accessibility.

Tailor CTAs to Your Content: Tailor your CTAs to align with the content of your podcast episode. If you're discussing a particular topic or product, create a CTA that seamlessly integrates with that theme, ensuring relevance and a smooth transition for your audience.

Offer Exclusive Rewards: Incentivize action by offering exclusive rewards tied to your CTAs. Whether it's special discounts, bonus content, or entry into a giveaway, providing extra incentives makes taking action more appealing to your listeners.

Encourage Social Sharing: Encourage listeners to share your podcast or the CTA with their social networks. Word-of-mouth recommendations can significantly amplify your reach. Include a social-sharing element in your CTAs to harness the power of your audience's network.

Test and Iterate: Continuously test the effectiveness of your CTAs and be open to iteration. Monitor engagement metrics, gather listener feedback, and refine your CTAs based on the data. A data-driven approach allows you to optimize your calls-to-action for maximum impact.

Crafting compelling CTAs requires a strategic blend of clarity, persuasion, and relevance. By aligning your CTAs with the content of your podcast, creating a sense of urgency, and offering valuable incentives, you can inspire your audience to take immediate and meaningful actions.

7. <u>Utilize Visuals and Multimedia:</u> Supplement your audio promotion with visual content on your podcast's website or social media platforms. This could include product images, infographics, or video demonstrations to enhance the promotional impact.

It is a powerful strategy to enhance engagement and provide a more comprehensive experience for your audience.

Here's how to effectively integrate visual elements:

> *<u>Create Visually Appealing Graphics:</u>* Design eye-catching graphics that represent your podcast episodes and promotions. Incorporate elements such as episode titles, guest names, and promotional details. Consistent and visually appealing graphics help establish a recognizable brand identity for your podcast.

> *<u>Utilize Episode Thumbnails:</u>* Design unique episode thumbnails for each podcast episode. These thumbnails can be shared on your website and social media platforms, serving as a visual preview of the episode's content. Thumbnails should be compelling and relevant, enticing listeners to explore the episode further.

> *<u>Share Behind-the-Scenes Content:</u>* Offer a glimpse behind the scenes by sharing photos or videos of your podcast recording sessions. This personal touch humanizes your podcast and allows your audience to connect with the creators. Post these visual snippets on social media platforms to build a more intimate relationship with

your listeners.

Visual Quotes and Highlights: Pull impactful quotes or highlights from your podcast episodes and transform them into visually appealing graphics. Share these graphics on social media platforms with a call-to-action encouraging listeners to tune in for more insightful content.

Promotional Banners on Your Website: Feature promotional banners on your podcast's website that highlight special offers, exclusive content, or upcoming episodes. Ensure these banners are prominently displayed to capture the attention of visitors and entice them to explore further.

Create Shareable Infographics: Condense key information, statistics, or highlights from your episodes into shareable infographics. These visually engaging assets can be shared on social media platforms to convey valuable content in a concise and appealing format.

Visual Teasers for New Episodes: Generate anticipation for upcoming episodes by sharing visual teasers on your website and social media platforms. Use intriguing visuals or short video clips to tease the content and encourage your audience to mark their calendars for the release.

Interactive Visual Content: Experiment with interactive visual content, such as polls, quizzes, or interactive stories on platforms like Instagram or Facebook.

Engaging your audience through interactive visuals enhances participation and creates a dynamic online community around your podcast.

Host Live Streams or Q&A Sessions: Host live video sessions on social media platforms where you discuss podcast highlights, answer audience questions, or provide additional insights. Live visuals allow for real-time interaction and create a sense of immediacy, fostering a deeper connection with your audience.

Consistent Branding Elements: Maintain consistency in branding elements across your visual content. Use consistent color schemes, fonts, and logos to reinforce your podcast's identity. A cohesive visual presence contributes to a professional and memorable brand image.

Encourage User-Generated Visuals: Encourage your audience to create and share their visual content related to your podcast. Whether it's fan art, memes, or creative interpretations, user-generated visuals contribute to a vibrant community and amplify your podcast's reach.

By integrating visual content into your podcast promotion strategy, you not only capture the attention of your audience but also provide additional layers of engagement. Visual elements enhance the overall storytelling experience and help build a stronger and more visually connected community around your podcast.

8. <u>Share Personal Testimonials:</u> Genuine endorsements based on real experiences can significantly influence your listeners' purchasing decisions.

If you have personal experience with affiliate products, sharing authentic testimonials with your audience can significantly enhance the credibility of your recommendations. When incorporating your personal experiences into your podcast, it's essential to strike a balance between enthusiasm and sincerity.

Begin by highlighting the specific ways in which the affiliate product has positively impacted your life or addressed a particular need. Speak to the features that impressed you and share any unique benefits you've personally enjoyed. By providing concrete examples, you not only showcase the product's functionality but also demonstrate its real-world application.

Avoid scripted or overly promotional language; instead, communicate in a conversational and relatable tone. Authenticity is key in building trust, and your audience is more likely to connect with genuine, unfiltered testimonials. If there were any challenges or limitations you encountered, don't hesitate to mention them, along with how you navigated or overcame them.

Consider weaving your personal testimonial seamlessly into the broader context of your podcast content. Whether it's during a dedicated product review segment or as part of a relevant discussion, the testimonial should feel like a natural extension of the conversation.

Furthermore, express gratitude for the positive impact the affiliate product has had on your life. This not only reinforces your endorsement but also conveys your sincerity and appreciation for products that genuinely contribute to your well-being.

Remember, your personal experiences and testimonials serve as valuable insights for your audience. By openly sharing your authentic thoughts, you contribute to a more informed and trusting relationship with your listeners, strengthening the connection between you, the products you endorse, and your audience.

9. Leverage Social Media Platforms: Extend your affiliate promotion efforts to social media platforms. Create engaging posts, stories, or live sessions to reach a broader audience and drive traffic to your affiliate links.

Creating engaging posts, stories, or live sessions is a dynamic approach to reach a broader audience and drive traffic to your affiliate links. *To maximize impact, consider the following strategies:*

> *Start by Understanding Your Audience:* Before crafting content, understand your audience's preferences, interests, and behaviors. Tailor your posts to resonate with their needs and desires, ensuring that your content aligns with their expectations.

> *Leverage Visually Appealing Content:* Visuals are powerful tools to capture attention. Create eye-catching graphics,

images, or short videos that highlight the key features and benefits of the affiliate products. Use aesthetically pleasing visuals to stand out in crowded social media feeds.

Craft Compelling Headlines and Captions: Write compelling headlines and captions that spark curiosity and encourage engagement. Pose questions, share intriguing insights, or leverage storytelling techniques to draw your audience in. Make it clear how the affiliate product can add value to their lives.

Utilize Storytelling in Live Sessions: When hosting live sessions, incorporate storytelling to make the content more relatable and engaging. Share personal anecdotes about how the affiliate product has positively impacted your life, creating a narrative that resonates with your audience.

Employ a Mix of Content Formats: Diversify your content by using various formats, such as images, videos, carousels, and infographics. Different content formats cater to different audience preferences and can enhance the overall viewing experience.

Create Tutorials or Demonstrations: Showcase the practical use of affiliate products through tutorials or demonstrations. Whether it's a step-by-step guide or a live demonstration, illustrating how the product solves a problem or enhances an experience can be compelling for your audience.

Encourage Audience Participation: Foster engagement by encouraging your audience to participate in your content. Pose questions, run polls, or ask for their opinions on the featured products. Actively responding to comments and messages enhances the sense of community around your content.

Promote Limited-Time Offers: Instill a sense of urgency by promoting limited-time offers or exclusive deals tied to your affiliate links. Highlighting time-sensitive promotions creates a compelling reason for your audience to take immediate action.

Use Hashtags Strategically: Leverage relevant hashtags to increase the discoverability of your content. Research and use popular hashtags related to your niche and the affiliate products you're promoting. This can expose your content to a wider audience interested in similar topics.

Cross-Promote on Different Platforms: Extend your reach by cross-promoting your affiliate content on various social media platforms. Each platform has its unique audience, and cross-promotion ensures that your content is seen by a diverse range of users.

Measure and Optimize: Regularly analyze the performance of your content using analytics tools. Understand which posts or sessions resonate most with your audience and optimize your approach accordingly. Data-driven insights allow you to refine your content strategy for better results.

By adopting these strategies, you can create engaging and impactful content that not only reaches a broader audience but also effectively drives traffic to your affiliate links. Remember to adapt your approach based on the evolving preferences of your audience and the dynamics of each social media platform.

10. <u>Track and Analyze Performance:</u> Effectively utilizing tracking tools provided by affiliate programs is crucial for monitoring the performance of your promotions and assessing the effectiveness of your efforts.

Here's a guide on how to leverage these tools:

<u>*Implement Tracking Pixels or Codes:*</u> Many affiliate programs offer tracking pixels or unique affiliate codes that can be integrated into the links you share. Implement these tracking elements on your website, blog, or social media platforms to monitor user interactions and conversions accurately.

<u>*Monitor Click-through Rates (CTR):*</u> Tracking tools provide insights into the number of clicks your affiliate links receive. Monitor the click-through rates (CTR) to understand how often your audience engages with the promoted products. A high CTR indicates strong interest and engagement.

<u>*Analyze Conversion Rates:*</u> Conversion rates are a key

metric for assessing the success of your affiliate promotions. Track the number of clicks that result in actual conversions, whether it's a sale, sign-up, or another predefined action. Analyzing conversion rates helps you identify the most effective promotional strategies.

Examine User Behavior: Utilize tracking tools to examine user behavior after clicking on your affiliate links. Understand which pages they visit, how long they stay, and whether they complete the desired actions. This information helps you identify potential areas for optimization in your promotional funnel.

Segment and Target Specific Audiences: Some tracking tools allow you to segment your audience based on various criteria, such as demographics or location. Leverage this feature to identify high-performing audience segments. Tailor your future promotions to target these specific groups more effectively.

Track Revenue and Earnings: Monitor the revenue generated from your affiliate promotions. Tracking tools often provide real-time data on earnings, giving you immediate insights into the financial impact of your efforts. This information is valuable for assessing the overall success of your affiliate marketing strategy.

Utilize UTM Parameters: Implement UTM parameters in your affiliate links to track the source of clicks accurately. This is particularly useful for understanding which marketing channels or campaigns are driving the most traffic and conversions. Adjust your promotional efforts based on this data to optimize performance.

Set Goals and Benchmarks: Establish clear goals and benchmarks for your affiliate promotions. Whether it's achieving a certain conversion rate, reaching a specific revenue target, or increasing overall clicks, having measurable objectives allows you to gauge the success of your campaigns.

Regularly Review and Optimize: Schedule regular reviews of your tracking data to identify patterns and trends. Analyze which strategies are delivering the best results and optimize your approach accordingly. Continuous monitoring and optimization are essential for long-term success in affiliate marketing.

Communicate with Affiliate Managers: Engage with affiliate program managers to gain additional insights and advice. They can provide guidance on optimizing your promotional efforts based on the tracking data. Building a collaborative relationship with program managers enhances your overall affiliate marketing strategy.

By actively utilizing tracking tools and analyzing relevant metrics, you gain valuable insights into the performance of your affiliate promotions. This data-driven approach empowers you to make informed decisions, refine your strategies, and maximize the impact of your affiliate marketing efforts.

11. <u>Rotate and Refresh Promotions</u>: To keep your content fresh and maintain the interest of your audience, it's essential to periodically introduce new affiliate products or refresh your promotions. This prevents listener fatigue and ensures ongoing interest in your recommendations.

Here's a guide on how to effectively achieve this:

<u>Stay Informed About Trends:</u> Regularly stay informed about industry trends, emerging products, and changes in consumer preferences. By staying up-to-date, you can identify new affiliate products that align with current interests, ensuring your content remains relevant.

<u>Rotate Featured Products:</u> Instead of exclusively promoting a single affiliate product for an extended period, consider rotating featured products. Introduce variety by showcasing different products, services, or brands over time. This approach keeps your content dynamic and prevents monotony.

<u>Align with Seasonal Themes:</u> Capitalize on seasonal themes or events to introduce new affiliate products. Whether it's holiday promotions, back-to-school offers, or seasonal trends, aligning your promotions with relevant themes adds a timely and engaging element to your content.

<u>Highlight Limited-Time Offers:</u> Introduce a sense of urgency by highlighting limited-time offers or exclusive promotions. Create a sense of excitement by periodically

featuring time-sensitive deals, encouraging your audience to act quickly. Limited-time promotions can reignite interest and drive immediate engagement.

Conduct Product Reviews or Comparisons: Periodically conduct in-depth product reviews or comparisons. This not only introduces new products to your audience but also provides valuable insights for informed decision-making. Share your personal experiences with the products to add authenticity to your recommendations.

Collaborate with New Affiliates: Explore collaborations with new affiliates or partners. This not only diversifies the range of products you can promote but also introduces your audience to different brands and offerings. Collaborations can bring a fresh perspective and broaden the appeal of your content.

Introduce Exclusive Deals for Your Audience: Negotiate exclusive deals or discounts with affiliate partners specifically for your audience. Introducing exclusive offers enhances the value proposition for your listeners and motivates them to explore and engage with the new promotions you present.

Utilize Different Content Formats: Experiment with different content formats when introducing new affiliate products. Whether it's creating unboxing videos, tutorials, or interactive content, varying your content formats keeps your audience engaged and excited about your promotions.

Seek Feedback from Your Audience: Actively seek feedback from your audience about the types of products they are interested in. This can be done through surveys, polls, or direct interactions on social media. Tailor your promotions based on the preferences and needs expressed by your audience.

Refresh Existing Content: Refresh and repurpose existing content by providing updates or additional information about previously promoted products. Share new use cases, features, or improvements to keep the content relevant and showcase the enduring value of the products.

Maintain Consistency in Branding: While introducing new products, maintain consistency in branding. Ensure that the new affiliate products align with your overall content strategy and resonate with your brand image. Consistency builds trust and familiarity with your audience.

By thoughtfully integrating affiliate product promotions into your podcast, you can create a win-win situation for both you and your audience while building a sustainable stream of revenue.

CHAPTER 4

Listener Donations

*E*ncourage listener support through platforms like Patreon or Buy Me a Coffee. Offer exclusive content or perks to those who contribute.

Securing listener donations for your podcast can be a rewarding way to support your content and engage with your audience.

Here are some strategies to encourage listener donations:

1. <u>Express the Need:</u> Clearly communicate the need for listener support. Share information about the costs associated with producing and maintaining your podcast, including hosting fees, equipment expenses, and time invested. When listeners understand the financial challenges, they may be more willing to contribute.

Let's explore an example of how a podcast host, named Alex, clearly communicates the need for listener support in order to cover the costs associated with producing and maintaining the podcast.

Podcast: Mindful Musings with Alex

Hello, Mindful Tribe! This is Alex, the host of "Mindful Musings," and I wanted to take a moment to have an open and honest conversation with all of you, our incredible listeners.

Producing "Mindful Musings" has been an incredibly rewarding journey, and your support has made it all possible. However, as the podcast continues to grow, so do the costs associated with creating and maintaining each episode.

1. Hosting Fees:

Hosting our episodes online and ensuring they're available for you to stream or download comes with monthly hosting fees. This is like the rent we pay to have a space on the internet where our episodes can live.

2. Quality Equipment:

Investing in quality recording equipment and software allows us to deliver the best audio experience possible. This ensures that each episode is clear, engaging, and enjoyable for you, our amazing listeners.

3. Editing and Production:

Crafting each episode involves hours of editing and production to bring you content that is polished and professional. Your support helps us compensate the talented individuals who work behind the scenes to make each episode seamless.

4. Research and Development:

We're committed to bringing you thought-provoking and insightful content. Researching topics, interviewing guests, and staying up-to-date with the latest in our field all require time and resources.

5. Time Investment:

As much as I love creating content for "Mindful Musings," *it's essential to acknowledge the time invested. Your contributions allow me to dedicate the necessary time to deliver quality episodes consistently.*

I want to be transparent with you all. The financial challenges associated with running a podcast are real, and that's why I'm reaching out to our incredible community. If "Mindful Musings" *has added value to your life, if our discussions have sparked inspiration or offered moments of reflection, I kindly ask for your support.*

Whether it's a one-time contribution or becoming a monthly supporter, every bit counts. Your support will directly contribute to the continued growth and sustainability of "Mindful Musings." *Head over to our website or check out the support link in the show notes to find out how you can be part of keeping the mindful conversations alive.*

Thank you for being a part of our community and for considering supporting "Mindful Musings." *Together, we can ensure that these meaningful conversations continue to reach hearts and minds around the world.*

Wishing you all mindfulness and gratitude,

Alex

This example illustrates how a podcast host can openly communicate the financial challenges associated with producing a podcast and make a compelling case for listener support. Transparency and sincerity in sharing the specific costs and time invested can foster a sense of community and encourage listeners to contribute.

2. <u>Offer Value-Added Content:</u> Create exclusive content or perks for donors. This could include bonus episodes, early access to new content, behind-the-scenes insights, or special shout-outs in your episodes. Providing additional value makes the donation more enticing for your audience.

Let's explore an example of how a podcaster, *Sarah*, creates exclusive content and perks for donors to enhance the appeal of supporting her podcast.

Podcast: Creative Canvas Unleashed with Sarah

Hello, Creative Souls! It's Sarah, *your host from* "Creative Canvas Unleashed," *and I have some exciting news to share with you.*

As you know, bringing you inspiring and thought-provoking content is my passion. To continue doing so, I'm reaching out to our amazing community for support. Your contribution can now come with some fantastic perks to make your donation even more special!

1. Bonus Episodes:

By becoming a donor, you'll gain access to exclusive bonus episodes that dive deeper into the creative process. These episodes will feature extended interviews, additional insights, and behind-the-scenes moments you won't find anywhere else.

2. Early Access to New Content:

Donors will be the first to experience new episodes before they are officially released to the public. Get a sneak peek into upcoming interviews, discussions, and explorations in the world of creativity.

3. Behind-the-Scenes Insights:

Ever wondered what happens behind the mic? Donors will receive exclusive behind-the-scenes content, including bloopers, outtakes, and glimpses into the making of each episode. It's like having a backstage pass to the Creative Canvas Unleashed experience!

4. Personalized Shout-Outs:

As a token of my gratitude, donors will receive personalized shout-outs in episodes. Your support is the lifeblood of this podcast, and I want the world to know how much you mean to the Creative Canvas Unleashed community.

5. Interactive Q&A Sessions:

Enjoy exclusive access to live Q&A sessions where you can ask me questions, share your thoughts, and engage in direct conversations about creativity, art, and the podcast.

6. Exclusive Merchandise Discounts:

Donors will also receive special discounts on Creative Canvas Unleashed merchandise. Wear your creativity proudly with unique items inspired by the podcast.

Becoming a donor is not just about supporting the podcast; it's about joining a community of like-minded individuals who appreciate and celebrate the beauty of creativity.

Visit our website or check out the donation link in the show notes to unlock these exclusive perks and become a vital part of the Creative Canvas Unleashed family. Your support ensures that we continue to explore, inspire, and unleash the limitless potential of the creative mind.

Thank you for being the driving force behind Creative Canvas Unleashed. Let's continue this artistic journey together!

Creatively yours,

Sarah

This example illustrates how a podcaster can entice audience support by offering exclusive content and personalized perks, creating a sense of community and appreciation for donors of the "Creative Canvas Unleashed" podcast.

3. <u>Choose a Reliable Payment Platform:</u> Set up a reliable and user-friendly payment platform to facilitate donations. Popular options include Patreon, Ko-fi, Buy Me a Coffee, or even direct contributions through platforms like PayPal or Venmo. Make the donation process simple and secure to encourage participation.

Let's explore an example of how a podcaster, Mark, sets up a reliable and user-friendly payment platform to facilitate donations for his podcast, "TechTalk Insights."

Podcast: TechTalk Insights with Mark

Hello, TechTalk community! It's Mark, your host from "TechTalk Insights." I'm thrilled to share some exciting news about how you can directly support the show and be an integral part of shaping its future.

1. Introducing our Donation Platform:

To make supporting "TechTalk Insights" easy and convenient, we've set up a user-friendly donation platform. Whether you're a long-time listener or a new member of our community, your contributions play a vital role in fueling the growth of the podcast.

2. Options to Fit Your Preference:

We understand that everyone has their preferred way of supporting content creators. That's why we offer multiple options, including Patreon, Ko-fi, and Buy Me a Coffee. If you prefer, you can also make direct contributions through platforms like PayPal or Venmo.

3. Patreon:

For those who want to make ongoing monthly contributions and enjoy exclusive perks, our Patreon page is the perfect place to be. Unlock bonus content, early access, and special shout-outs by becoming a TechTalk Patron.

4. Ko-fi and Buy Me a Coffee:

If you'd rather make one-time contributions or buy us a virtual coffee to show your support, Ko-fi and Buy Me a Coffee are fantastic options. Every gesture, big or small, makes a significant impact on keeping the podcast running.

5. Secure and Simple Process:

We've prioritized the security of your transactions, and the donation process is designed to be simple and hassle-free. Just head to our website, click on the "Support" tab, and choose the platform that suits you best. A few clicks, and you're done!

6. Regular Updates and Thank-Yous:

I believe in keeping you informed about how your contributions are making a difference. Regular updates and special thank-you messages will be shared with our generous supporters, ensuring you're always in the loop.

7. Exclusive Access for Supporters:

As a token of gratitude, supporters will gain access to exclusive content, sneak peeks into upcoming episodes, and even have a say in the topics we cover. Your support goes beyond just a donation; it's a partnership in shaping the future of "TechTalk Insights."

Your contributions enable us to bring you high-quality content, exciting interviews, and insightful discussions about the world of technology. Visit our website today to support "TechTalk Insights" and be part of our tech-loving community.

> *Thank you for powering the insights and conversations that matter in the tech world.*
>
> *Tech on,*
>
> Mark

This example demonstrates how a podcaster can communicate the donation options clearly, providing choices that suit different preferences while emphasizing simplicity and security in the process.

4. Highlight Listener Contributions: Regularly acknowledge and thank donors on your podcast. Mentioning their names or messages in episodes shows appreciation and reinforces the sense of community. This recognition can motivate others to contribute as well.

Let's explore an example of how a podcaster, Rachel, regularly acknowledges and thanks donors on her podcast, "Mindful Moments with Rachel."

Podcast: Mindful Moments with Rachel

> *Hello, Mindful Community! It's Rachel, your guide on this journey of self-discovery and mindfulness. Today, I want to express my deepest gratitude to some incredible individuals who have supported "Mindful Moments" through their generous contributions.*

1. Heartfelt Shout-Outs:

Before we dive into today's mindful topic, I want to take a moment to send some love and appreciation to our amazing donors. Your support keeps the mindful conversations flowing, and I'm truly grateful for each and every one of you.

2. Personalized Thank-Yous:

Special thanks to Sarah, who recently became a monthly supporter on our Patreon page. Your commitment to the podcast means the world to me, Sarah. I appreciate you being part of our mindful community.

3. Messages from the Community:

We also have a beautiful message from John, who made a generous contribution on Ko-fi. John writes, "Mindful Moments has been a guiding light in my daily routine. Grateful to be part of this community." Thank you, John, for your kind words and support.

4. Expressing Impact:

Your contributions allow us to explore new topics, bring on inspiring guests, and continue creating content that nourishes the soul. Each donation is a vote of confidence, and it propels "Mindful Moments" forward.

5. Inviting Others to Join:

If you're finding value in our mindful discussions and

want to join the incredible individuals we've acknowledged today, head over to our website or check the show notes for ways to support the podcast. Your contribution, whether big or small, makes a meaningful impact.

6. Listener Spotlight:

In our next episode, we'll be featuring a "Listener Spotlight" segment where I'll be sharing insights and reflections from members of our mindful community. If you'd like to be featured or have a message you'd like to share, let me know!

Remember, "Mindful Moments" is not just my podcast; it's our mindful community. Your support, whether through donations, messages, or simply being a part of the audience, makes this community thrive.

Thank you for your generosity, your presence, and your commitment to mindful living. Now, let's embark on another journey of self-discovery together.

Mindfully yours,

Rachel

This example demonstrates how a podcaster can regularly acknowledge and thank donors on the podcast, creating a sense of community, and showcasing the impact of their support. Recognition like this not only expresses gratitude but also motivates others to contribute to the community.

5. **<u>Set Clear Goals:</u>** Establish clear and achievable donation goals. Whether it's covering monthly hosting fees, upgrading equipment, or funding special projects, clearly outline how listener donations will be utilized. This transparency helps build trust with your audience.

Let's explore an example of how a podcaster, Alex, establishes clear and achievable donation goals for his podcast, "Adventures Unbound."

Podcast: Adventures Unbound with Alex

Hello, Adventurers! It's Alex, your fellow wanderer and the host of "Adventures Unbound." Today, I'm excited to share with you some transparent and exciting updates about the future of our podcast and how your support can play a crucial role.

1. Monthly Hosting Fees:

Our first goal is to cover the monthly hosting fees for "Adventures Unbound." Your donations will ensure that we can continue delivering high-quality episodes without interruption. Our aim is to create a seamless listening experience for you.

2. Equipment Upgrades:

As we embark on more adventures, it's essential to enhance our equipment for better audio quality and immersive storytelling. Donations will contribute to upgrading our recording gear, ensuring that each episode feels like a journey unfolding right before your ears.

3. Special Project Fund:

Ever dreamt of a unique adventure series, perhaps with on-location recordings or collaborations with fellow adventurers? We do too! Your support will help fund special projects that go beyond our regular episodes, making our podcast even more captivating and memorable.

4. Listener-Requested Content:

We've received fantastic suggestions from our listeners about topics they'd love us to explore. Meeting our donation goals will enable us to prioritize and create content based on your interests and requests.

5. Achievable Milestones:

To keep it transparent, we've set achievable milestones. Once we reach a specific donation level, we'll celebrate with bonus episodes, exclusive content, or even live Q&A sessions. Your support directly unlocks these exciting rewards for the entire Adventures Unbound community.

6. Regular Updates and Progress Reports:

I believe in keeping you informed about how your contributions are making a difference. Regular updates and progress reports will be shared, showcasing the impact your donations have on the podcast's growth.

7. Building Trust Together:

Establishing clear and achievable goals is about building trust with our incredible community. Your support isn't just about financial contributions; it's about collectively shaping the future of "Adventures Unbound."

8. How You Can Contribute:

Visit our website or check the show notes for a link to our donation page. There, you'll find details about our goals, progress, and the different ways you can contribute. Every contribution, no matter the size, brings us closer to new horizons.

Thank you for being a part of our adventures. Together, we'll unlock new chapters, explore uncharted territories, and make "Adventures Unbound" an even more incredible journey.

Happy adventuring,

Alex

This example demonstrates how a podcaster can establish clear and achievable donation goals, outlining how listener contributions will be utilized to enhance the podcast's quality, create special projects, and align with the interests of the community. Transparency builds trust and motivates listeners to actively support the podcast.

6. <u>Promote Donation Drives:</u> Periodically run donation drives or campaigns. Create a sense of urgency by tying these campaigns to specific milestones, events, or improvements you want to make to the podcast. Encourage your audience to participate and share the campaign with others.

Below is an example of how you would structure a message for periodically running donation drives or campaigns for your podcast, creating a sense of urgency and encouraging audience participation:

📢 [*Your Podcast Name*] Community Update: Help Us Reach New Heights! 🚀

Dear [Podcast Community],

We hope this message finds you well and filled with the same excitement that we have as we continue to grow together in the [Your Podcast Name] *family! Your support has been phenomenal, and we're eager to take our podcast to new heights.*

🌟 Why We Need Your Help:

As we strive to enhance your listening experience, we've set ambitious goals for the next chapter of [Your Podcast Name]. *We're looking to upgrade our equipment, bring in expert guests, and explore innovative content ideas that will captivate your ears and minds even more.*

🔔 The Countdown Begins:

To make all this happen, we're launching a special donation drive starting [Campaign Start Date] *and ending* [Campaign End Date]. *This is a limited-time opportunity for you to contribute directly to the growth of* [Your Podcast Name] *and be a crucial part of our journey.*

⏰ Sense of Urgency:

But here's the catch — we've tied this campaign to a specific milestone. Our goal is to reach [Specific Fundraising Target] *by* [Campaign End Date]. *This will enable us to implement the upgrades and enhancements we've been dreaming of for months.*

🌐 How You Can Contribute:

- *Visit our dedicated donation page at* [Donation Page Link].
- *Choose from a range of contribution options that suit your comfort.*
- *Share our campaign on social media using* #Support[YourPodcastName] *to create a ripple effect.*

🛡 Exclusive Perks for Contributors:

To show our gratitude, we've prepared special perks for those who contribute:

- *Personalized shoutouts in our upcoming episodes.*
- *Exclusive behind-the-scenes content.*
- *Limited edition* [Your Podcast Name] *merchandise for top contributors.*

💡 Spread the Word:

Help us create a buzz! Share our campaign with your friends, family, and fellow podcast enthusiasts. Every share counts and brings us one step closer to our goal.

🙏 Thank You for Being Amazing:

We wouldn't be where we are without your incredible support. Thank you for being an integral part of the [Your Podcast Name] *community. Let's reach new heights together!*

With gratitude,

[Your Name]

[Your Podcast Name]

Feel free to customize this template according to your podcast's style and specific goals.

7. Incorporate Calls-to-Action (CTAs): Include calls-to-action in your podcast episodes, website, and social media platforms. Remind your audience about the option to support the podcast through donations and provide clear instructions on how to do so. Regularly reinforce this message to keep it top of mind.

Below is an example of how you can incorporate calls-to-action in your podcast episodes, website, and social media platforms to remind your audience about supporting your podcast through donations:

🎙️ [Your Podcast Name] Support Campaign: Your Voice, Your Support! 🌟

Podcast Episode CTA:

[Podcast Intro]

🎤 Host: *Hey, [Your Podcast Name] family! Before we dive into today's episode, we want to take a quick moment to express our gratitude for your incredible support. Your enthusiasm keeps us going!*

✒️ Host: *If you love what we do and want to be a crucial part of our journey, consider supporting [Your Podcast Name]. Your contributions make a significant impact and help us bring you even more amazing content.*

🚀 Host: *Interested in supporting? Head over to [Donation Page Link] to make a donation. Every little bit counts, and we appreciate each and every one of you!*

[Podcast Content]

[Podcast Outro]

🔗 **Website CTA:**

[Homepage Banner]

🌐 **Banner Text:** *Love [Your Podcast Name]? Support us and help us grow! Click here to make a donation.*

[Support Page]

📍 **Support Page Text:** *Your support means the world to us! If you enjoy [Your Podcast Name] and want to contribute, please consider making a donation. Your generosity fuels our passion for creating great content.*

[Clear Donation Instructions]

Click the "Donate Now" button.
Choose your preferred contribution amount.
Complete the simple form to finalize your donation.

📢 Social Media CTA:

🌟 Twitter Post:

Hey [Your Podcast Name] fans! 🎧 *Your support keeps our podcast alive and thriving.* 🚀 *If you love what we do, consider making a donation and being a part of our journey! Click here to support: [Donation Page Link] #Support[YourPodcastName]*

📓 Instagram Post:

Swipe left to see how you can support [Your Podcast Name]! Your donations help us create more content for you. 📢 *Visit our profile and click the link in bio to make a difference.* 🙌 *#PodcastLove #SupportUs*

📌 Regular Reinforcement:

- Weekly Reminders: *Include a short reminder in your weekly social media posts about supporting the podcast.*
- Thank You Shoutouts: *Regularly thank your donors in your episodes. It not only shows appreciation but also reinforces the idea that support is crucial.*

Remember, consistency is key! Keep the message clear and enthusiastic to encourage your audience to take action and support your podcast.

Feel free to adjust the language and details to better fit your podcast's unique style and voice.

8. <u>Share Personal Stories:</u> Share personal stories about why your podcast is meaningful to you and how listener support can make a difference. Connecting on a personal level can resonate with your audience and inspire them to contribute.

Here are 2 examples of scripts you may use in your podcast.

<u>SCRIPT #1</u>

As the creator and host of [Your Podcast Name], I wanted to take a moment to share a personal story about why this podcast is so meaningful to me. When I started this journey, I had a vision of creating a space where people could connect, learn, and be inspired. Little did I know how profoundly this podcast would impact both my life and the lives of our listeners.

One of the most heartwarming aspects of running [Your Podcast Name] has been the incredible stories and messages I receive from listeners. Hearing about how an episode sparked a positive change, provided comfort during a tough time, or simply brought joy to someone's day is beyond fulfilling. It's these moments that make all the hard work worthwhile.

Now, I want to invite you to be a part of this journey in a more tangible way. Listener support can make a genuine difference in the growth and sustainability of [Your Podcast Name]. It allows us to continue producing content that resonates with you and others around the world. Your contribution isn't just financial; it's a vote of confidence, a way of saying, "I believe in the impact of this podcast."

Imagine the ripple effect — by supporting [Your Podcast Name], you're not just supporting me as the host; you're supporting a community that values learning, growth, and shared experiences. Your generosity enables us to bring in expert guests, improve production quality, and explore new topics that matter to you.

So, if you've ever found solace, inspiration, or a sense of belonging through [Your Podcast Name], I invite you to consider making a contribution. Visit our donation page at [YourPodcastWebsite.com/Donate], and know that your support goes directly towards making this podcast even more meaningful for you and the entire community.

Thank you for being a part of this incredible journey. Your support, in whatever form, is a beacon of encouragement that keeps [Your Podcast Name] shining bright.

With gratitude,

[Your Name]

Host, [Your Podcast Name]

SCRIPT # 2

Hey [Your Podcast Community]!

I wanted to take a moment today to share a personal story about why [Your Podcast Name] holds a special place in my heart and why your support means the world to me.

When I started this podcast, it was driven by a passion to create a space for meaningful conversations and shared experiences. What I didn't anticipate was the incredible community that would form around it. Your messages, stories, and the connections forged through [Your Podcast Name] have been nothing short of extraordinary.

One particular story stands out. I received a heartfelt message from a listener who shared how an episode about overcoming challenges resonated deeply during a tough period in their life. It reminded me of the incredible impact podcasts can have on individuals, providing comfort and companionship during difficult times.

This is why your support is so crucial. It goes beyond just keeping the podcast running; it enables us to continue producing content that genuinely matters. Your contribution is an investment in the shared moments, insights, and emotions that make [Your Podcast Name] what it is.

I've always believed in the power of storytelling, and it's your stories, shared and lived, that fuel the essence of this podcast. So, I want to extend an invitation to be a more active part of this journey. By supporting [Your Podcast Name], you're not just backing a show; you're supporting a community of like-minded individuals who find meaning, inspiration, and joy in the stories we tell.

Whether it's the uplifting interviews, the insightful discussions, or the occasional moments of laughter, your support ensures we can continue delivering content that resonates with you. If [Your Podcast Name] has touched your life in any way, I invite you to consider contributing. Visit our donation page at [YourPodcastWebsite.com/Donate], and know that your support directly contributes to the stories we share and the community we've built together.

Thank you for being a part of this journey and for considering supporting [Your Podcast Name]. Your generosity makes a difference, and I'm excited to see how we can continue growing and evolving together.

With gratitude,

[Your Name]

Host, [Your Podcast Name]

9. Offer Merchandise as Rewards: Use merchandise as a reward for donations. Offer exclusive items such as branded T-shirts, mugs, or stickers to donors. This not only provides tangible value but also serves as a token of appreciation for their support.

Here are a few examples.

🎉 Support [Your Podcast Name] and Get Exclusive Merch! 🌟

Dear [Your Podcast Name] Community,

We're beyond grateful for the incredible support you've shown [Your Podcast Name]! Your enthusiasm keeps us motivated, and we wanted to find a special way to say thank you.

Introducing our exclusive donation rewards program! Now, when you contribute to [Your Podcast Name], you not only support the podcast's growth but also get your hands on some awesome, limited-edition merchandise.

👕 [Your Podcast Name] Branded T-Shirt:

For a donation of $30 or more, you'll receive our exclusive [Your Podcast Name] T-shirt. It's not just a piece of clothing; it's a symbol of your commitment to our podcast community.

☕ [Your Podcast Name] Mug:

With a donation of $20 or more, you can enjoy your favorite beverage in our custom [Your Podcast Name] mug. It's the perfect way to start your day and show off your podcast pride.

🎨 [Your Podcast Name] Sticker Pack:

A donation of $10 or more earns you our vibrant sticker pack. Stick them on your laptop, water bottle, or anywhere you want to share your love for [Your Podcast Name].

♥ Why Merchandise?

We believe in giving back, and these items aren't just merchandise — they're tokens of our appreciation. They represent the shared moments, laughter, and learning that make [Your Podcast Name] special.

⊕ How to Get Your Merch:

Visit our donation page at [YourPodcastWebsite.com/Donate].
Choose your donation amount.
Select your preferred merch reward.
Complete the donation process, and we'll handle the rest!

⬟ Exclusive Perks for Top Contributors:

As a special thank you to our top contributors, we'll feature your name in an upcoming episode and send you a personalized thank-you video from the host!

Your support means the world to us, and we can't wait to see you rocking [Your Podcast Name] gear. Thank you for being a crucial part of our journey!

With gratitude,

[Your Name]

Host, [Your Podcast Name]

P.S. Limited quantities are available, so don't miss out on your chance to grab these exclusive items!

10. <u>Engage with Your Community:</u> Foster a strong community around your podcast through social media groups, forums, or other platforms. Actively engage with your audience, respond to their comments, and create a sense of belonging. A supportive community is more likely to contribute financially. Following are the examples.

🌐 Join the [Your Podcast Name] Community: Where Conversations Thrive! 🚀

Hey [*Your Podcast Name*] enthusiasts!

We're excited to invite you to join the thriving [*Your Podcast Name*] community, a space where the magic of our podcast comes to life beyond the episodes. Whether you're a long-time listener or just discovering us, this community is all about connecting, sharing, and growing together.

👥 Why Join?

> Engage in Discussions: Dive deep into podcast topics, share your insights, and connect with fellow enthusiasts. Your thoughts could spark a whole new conversation!

> Exclusive Content: Get sneak peeks, behind-the-scenes content, and special announcements before anyone else. You're the first to know what's happening in the [Your Podcast Name] world.

> Connect with Like-Minded People: Build connections with people who share your interests. Whether it's a favorite episode, a powerful message, or a shared experience, this is

the place to find your podcast tribe.

💬 Where to Join:

📱 Facebook Group: [*Your Podcast Name*] Community - Join the conversation on Facebook! Share your thoughts, connect with others, and be part of the family. [Link to Facebook Group]

🌐 Official Forum: Our dedicated forum is a hub for discussions. Visit [*YourPodcastForum.com*] and become part of a community that's passionate about the topics we explore.

🐦 Twitter Chats: Follow us on Twitter [*@YourPodcastHandle*] for live discussions, Q&A sessions, and more. Use *#YourPodcastCommunity* to join the conversation.

👀 Instagram Highlights: Explore our Instagram highlights for exclusive content, community spotlights, and updates. Follow us at [*@YourPodcastHandle*].

✴️ How to Engage:

Share Your Thoughts: *Comment on our posts, share your favorite episodes, and let us know what topics resonate with you.*

Ask Questions: *Have burning questions or curious thoughts? Drop them in the group, and we might feature them in an upcoming episode!*

Connect Beyond the Podcast: *Share your own stories, experiences, or recommendations. The community is a space for diverse voices to be heard.*

🦇 Why a Strong Community Matters:

A supportive community is the heartbeat of [*Your Podcast Name*]. We believe in the power of shared experiences and collective wisdom. Engaging with our community not only enriches your podcast journey but also contributes to a sense of belonging.

And here's the exciting part – a strong community is more likely to contribute financially! Your support helps us keep the podcast going and growing.

So, what are you waiting for? Join the [*Your Podcast Name*] community today and be part of something special!

With podcast love,

[*Your Name*]

Host, [*Your Podcast Name*]

11. **Host Live Q&A or AMA Sessions:** Host live question-and-answer sessions or "Ask Me Anything" (AMA) events exclusively for donors. This creates an interactive experience and adds an extra layer of exclusivity for those who contribute. Following are the examples.

🎤 [*Your Podcast Name*] Exclusive AMA Event: Your Questions, Our Answers! 🌐

Hello, fantastic supporters of [*Your Podcast Name*]!

We're thrilled to announce a special event just for our generous donors – an exclusive "Ask Me Anything" (AMA) session with yours truly! 🌟 This is your chance to get behind the scenes, ask burning questions, and dive deep into the topics you love.

📓 Date & Time: [*Insert Date and Time*]

📍 Where: [*Virtual Platform - Zoom, YouTube Live, etc.*]

💡 Why an Exclusive AMA?

We believe in creating meaningful experiences for our supporters, and what better way to do that than with a live Q&A session? This event is our way of saying thank you for your invaluable contributions to [*Your Podcast Name*]. It's a chance to connect in real-time, share insights, and have a candid conversation about all things podcast-related.

🚀 How to Join:

Make a Donation: Visit [*YourPodcastWebsite.com/Donate*] and make a donation of any amount. Your generosity grants you exclusive access to the AMA event.

Receive Confirmation: *Once your donation is confirmed, you'll receive an email with the details on how to join the live event.*

Save the Date: *Mark your calendar for the AMA session, and get ready for an interactive and engaging experience!*

💡 What to Expect:

- Behind-the-Scenes Insights: I'll share exclusive details about upcoming episodes, behind-the-scenes stories, and what goes into the making of [*Your Podcast Name*].
- Personalized Answers: This is your opportunity to ask me anything – from podcasting tips to my favorite episodes. Your questions will shape the conversation!
- Community Interaction: Connect with other donors, share your thoughts, and be part of a vibrant community that values your support.

🐾 Special Surprise:

As a token of our appreciation, all attendees will receive an exclusive digital resource created just for this event. It's our way of saying thank you for being an integral part of the [*Your Podcast Name*] family.

⚡ Ready to Join?

Make your donation now, secure your spot, and let's make this AMA session a memorable experience for everyone involved! We can't wait to connect with you live.

Thank you for your continued support – you make [*Your Podcast Name*] possible!

With gratitude,

[*Your Name*]

Host, [*Your Podcast Name*]

12. <u>Provide Flexible Contribution Options:</u> Offer flexibility in donation amounts. Some listeners may prefer to make small, recurring donations, while others may opt for one-time contributions. Providing various options allows listeners to choose what suits their budget and preferences. Following are some examples.

🌟 Support [*Your Podcast Name*]: Your Contribution, Your Choice! 🌐

Dear [*Your Podcast Name*] Community,

We're excited to introduce flexible donation options, empowering you to choose how you want to support [*Your Podcast Name*]. Your contributions play a vital role in keeping the podcast going, and we want to make it easy for everyone to be a part of our journey.

🖋 Why Flexibility Matters:

We understand that each listener has their own budget and preferences. That's why we've designed our donation system to offer flexibility, ensuring that supporting [*Your Podcast Name*] is accessible to everyone.

💲 Donation Options:

Small Monthly Pledge: Support us with a recurring monthly donation as low as $5. Even a small contribution each month adds up and makes a significant impact.

One-Time Gift: Prefer making a one-time contribution? You can choose any amount that feels right for you. Every contribution, big or small, helps us create quality content.
Custom Amount: Have a specific amount in mind? Our custom donation option allows you to contribute any amount you're comfortable with.

🚀 How to Contribute:

Visit Our Donation Page: Go to [*YourPodcastWebsite.com/Donate*].
Select Your Preferred Option: Choose between a small monthly pledge, a one-time gift, or a custom amount.
Complete the Process: Follow the simple steps to finalize your donation. Your support is just a few clicks away!

⬤ Exclusive Perks for Donors:

- <u>Personalized Shoutouts:</u> Your name will be featured in an upcoming episode as a special thank you.
- <u>Exclusive Content Access:</u> Enjoy behind-the-scenes content, bonus episodes, and more.

⚡ Why Your Contribution Matters:

Your generosity fuels the growth of [*Your Podcast Name*]. It allows us to invest in better equipment, bring in expert guests, and explore new and exciting topics. By contributing, you become an essential part of the community that makes this podcast thrive.

Thank you for considering supporting [*Your Podcast Name*]. Your choice in how you contribute is deeply appreciated, and we're excited to continue this journey with you!

With gratitude,

[*Your Name*]

Host, [*Your Podcast Name*]

Remember to express genuine gratitude for any contributions you receive and consistently demonstrate the impact of listener donations on the continued success and improvement of your podcast. Building a supportive and engaged community is key to a successful listener donation program.

CHAPTER 5

Merchandising

Creating and selling branded merchandise related to your podcast can be a fantastic way to engage your audience, build brand loyalty, and generate additional revenue. Here's a step-by-step guide on how to create and sell podcast merchandise:

1. **<u>Define Your Brand Identity</u>:** Before creating merchandise, ensure you have a clear understanding of your podcast's brand identity. Identify key elements such as your logo, color scheme, and any memorable catch phrases or themes associated with your show.

Let's create a fictional podcast, *"Adventures Unheard,"* and go through the process of identifying key elements such as the logo, color scheme, and memorable catch phrases or themes:

1. *<u>Logo:</u>*

- *Podcast Theme:* "Adventures Unheard" is a podcast that explores hidden stories and untold tales from around the world.
- *Logo Concept:* A compass rose intertwined with a vintage microphone, symbolizing exploration and storytelling.
- *Colors:* Earthy tones like deep blue and antique gold to evoke a sense of mystery and adventure.

2. Color Scheme:

- ***Main Colors:***
  - ➢ *Deep Blue:* Represents the vastness of unexplored stories.
  - ➢ *Antique Gold:* Adds a touch of vintage elegance and intrigue.
- ***Accents:***
  - ➢ *Ivory:* Used sparingly for a clean and classic look.
  - ➢ *Forest Green:* Represents the richness of undiscovered narratives.

3. Memorable Catch Phrases or Themes:

- ***Catchphrase 1:*** "Unlock the Tales, Unleash the Unheard!"
  - This catchphrase encapsulates the essence of the podcast, encouraging listeners to explore untold stories with "Adventures Unheard."
- ***Catchphrase 2:*** "Where Legends Meet Reality"
  - Reflects the podcast's theme of blending mythical narratives with factual storytelling.
- ***Theme:*** Each episode follows a unique theme like "Forgotten Heroes," "Mystical Lands," or "Whispers of the Past."

4. Podcast Artwork:

- The podcast's cover art features the logo prominently, with the deep blue and antique gold colors setting the tone. Images of an ancient map, a hidden scroll, and subtle silhouettes of various landmarks further convey the spirit of adventure.

5. *Sample Episode Intro:*

- "Welcome to 'Adventures Unheard,' where every episode is a journey into the unknown. I'm your host, [Your Name], and together, we'll unravel stories that time forgot. Grab your metaphorical passport because, with us, you're in for an adventure that transcends borders!"

6. *Merchandise Concept:*

- ***T-shirt Design:*** A stylish T-shirt featuring the podcast logo on the front and the catchphrase "Unlock the Tales, Unleash the Unheard!" on the back.
- ***Mug Design:*** A vintage-style mug with the compass rose logo wrapping around, creating an immersive feel for those sipping on their favorite beverage.

By identifying these key elements, "*Adventures Unheard*" has a cohesive brand identity that can be applied across various platforms, creating a recognizable and immersive experience for its audience.

2. <u>Know Your Audience:</u> Understand your audience's preferences and demographics. Tailor your merchandise to resonate with their tastes and interests. Consider conducting surveys or seeking direct feedback to gather insights into what your audience would like to see in your merchandise.

Let's continue with our fictional podcast, "*Adventures Unheard*," and explore how to understand the audience's preferences and demographics to tailor merchandise accordingly:

1. *Audience Preferences:*

- ***Conducting Surveys:*** Create a survey asking listeners about their preferences. Include questions about their favorite podcast episodes, preferred merchandise types (*e.g., T-shirts, mugs, stickers*), and any specific themes or symbols they associate with the podcast.
- ***Social Media Polls:*** Use platforms like Twitter or Instagram to run polls. For example, ask, "What colors do you associate with 'Adventures Unheard'?" or "Which catchphrase resonates with you the most?"

2. *Demographics:*

- ***Collect Data:*** If possible, gather demographic data through analytics tools or listener surveys. Identify age groups, locations, and interests.
- ***Engage on Social Media:*** Observe your audience's interactions on social media. Engage in conversations, respond to comments, and get a sense of who your listeners are.

3. *Merchandise Tailoring:*

- ***Based on Survey Responses:***

- If the survey reveals a preference for T-shirts, focus on creating high-quality, comfortable shirts featuring the podcast's key elements.
- If stickers emerge as a popular choice, design a set of stickers incorporating the logo and catchphrases.

- ***Considering Demographics:***
  - If your audience is primarily young adults, consider incorporating modern design elements and bold colors into the merchandise.
  - If your audience is diverse, ensure that the merchandise reflects inclusivity and cultural sensitivity.

- ***Aligning with Interests:***
  - If your audience expresses a love for outdoor adventures, design merchandise that's travel-friendly, like a durable water bottle or an adventure-themed hoodie.
  - If many listeners express a fondness for history, consider merchandise that pays homage to ancient maps or historical symbols.

4. *Gathering Direct Feedback:*

- ***Engage in Conversations:*** Host live Q&A sessions or virtual meet-ups where you directly ask listeners about their preferences.
- ***Email Newsletter Surveys:*** Include a merchandise-focused survey in your email newsletters. Offer an incentive, like a chance to win exclusive merchandise, to encourage

participation.

5. *Implementing Feedback:*

- ***Iterate Designs:*** If the audience expresses a strong preference for certain colors or symbols, ensure that these elements are prominently featured in the merchandise designs.
- ***Prioritize Popular Choices:*** If a specific merchandise item emerges as a favorite, prioritize its production to meet the demand.

6. *Communication:*

- ***Transparent Communication:*** Keep your audience informed about the merchandise creation process. Share sneak peeks, design concepts, and involve them in decisions.
- ***Express Gratitude:*** Thank your audience for their valuable input and emphasize how their preferences have shaped the merchandise collection.

By actively seeking and incorporating audience feedback, "Adventures Unheard" can ensure that its merchandise not only aligns with the brand identity but also resonates deeply with the tastes and interests of its dedicated listeners. This approach fosters a sense of community and ensures that the merchandise becomes a cherished extension of the podcast experience.

3. Design Eye-Catching Merchandise: Create visually appealing designs for your merchandise. This could include incorporating your podcast logo, tagline, or any unique graphics associated with your show. If you're not a designer, consider hiring a professional or using online design tools to bring your vision to life.

Let's continue with our fictional podcast, "*Adventures Unheard*," and explore how to create visually appealing designs for its merchandise:

1. *Visual Elements:*

- **Podcast Logo:** Utilize the podcast's compass rose intertwined with a vintage microphone as a central visual element. Ensure the logo is prominent and instantly recognizable.
- **Tagline:** Incorporate the podcast's catchy tagline, "Unlock the Tales, Unleash the Unheard!" in a stylish font that complements the overall design.
- **Key Imagery:** Consider using visuals that evoke a sense of adventure, such as ancient maps, hidden scrolls, or mysterious landscapes.

2. *Colors:*

- **Main Colors:** Incorporate the deep blue and antique gold colors from the podcast's color scheme. Ensure these colors are used strategically to create a visually cohesive look.
- **Accent Colors:** Introduce accents of ivory and forest green to add depth and visual interest.

3. *Merchandise Types:*

- **T-Shirt Design:**
    - *Front:* Place the podcast logo at the

center or upper chest area, keeping it
visible. Consider adding a subtle,
textured background to enhance the
design.
- *Back:* Feature the tagline in an elegant
font, creating a captivating visual impact.
- **Mug Design:**
  - Wrap the compass rose logo around the
mug, ensuring it complements the
cylindrical shape. Use the deep blue and
antique gold colors for a sophisticated
look.
- **Sticker Set:**
  - Design a set of stickers with variations
of the podcast logo, catchphrases, and
key imagery. Ensure the stickers are
versatile, making them suitable for
laptops, water bottles, and more.

4. <u>*Professional Design Assistance:*</u>

- **Hire a Professional Designer:** If design isn't
your forte, consider hiring a professional
graphic designer. Provide them with the
podcast's branding guidelines, key elements, and
any specific preferences you have.
- **Online Design Tools:** Alternatively, use
user-friendly online design tools like Canva or
Adobe Spark. These platforms offer templates
and customizable elements to bring your vision
to life.

5. <u>*Iterative Design Process:*</u>

- ***Feedback Loops:*** Share initial design concepts with your community for feedback. Use social media or email newsletters to gather opinions and make iterative improvements.
- ***Incorporate Audience Suggestions:*** If your audience provides input on specific design elements, such as color preferences or additional imagery, consider implementing those suggestions.

6. *Quality Assurance:*

- ***Print Testing:*** Before finalizing merchandise production, print test samples to ensure colors, textures, and details translate well from digital to physical form.
- ***Sample Reviews:*** Personally review and approve samples to guarantee that the merchandise meets your visual expectations and aligns with your podcast's brand identity.

7. *Clear Communication:*

- ***Launch Teasers:*** Generate excitement by teasing merchandise designs before the official launch. Share sneak peeks and create anticipation among your audience.
- ***Transparency:*** Communicate openly about the design process, thanking your audience for their input and involvement.

By incorporating these elements and following a careful design process, "Adventures Unheard" can ensure that its merchandise not only reflects the podcast's brand identity but is also visually appealing and captivating for its audience.

4. <u>Choose Quality Products</u>: Select high-quality merchandise that aligns with your audience's preferences. Common podcast merchandise includes T-shirts, hoodies, mugs, stickers, and tote bags. Ensure that the chosen products are comfortable, durable, and well-suited for your branding.

Let's continue with our fictional podcast, "Adventures Unheard," and explore how to select high-quality merchandise that aligns with the audience's preferences:

1. *T-Shirts:*

- **Style:** *Choose a comfortable, classic-fit T-shirt that appeals to a broad audience.*
- **Material:** *Opt for a soft and breathable fabric, such as a cotton blend.*
- **Design Placement:** *Ensure the podcast logo is prominently placed on the front, and the tagline is featured on the back.*

2. *Hoodies:*

- **Style:** *Select a cozy and versatile hoodie suitable for various occasions.*
- **Material:** *Look for a high-quality blend that provides warmth without sacrificing comfort.*
- **Design Integration:** *Incorporate the podcast logo on the chest area and explore the use of key imagery on the back or sleeves for added visual appeal.*

3. *Mugs:*

- **Material:** *Choose durable ceramic mugs that can withstand regular use.*
- **Design Placement:** *Wrap the compass rose logo around the mug for an immersive effect.*
- **Color Options:** *Offer the mugs in colors that complement the podcast's color scheme, such as deep blue or antique gold.*

4. *Stickers:*

- **Material Quality:** *Opt for vinyl or waterproof material to ensure longevity.*
- **Variety:** *Create a set of stickers with different designs, including variations of the podcast logo, catchphrases, and key imagery.*
- **Versatility:** *Ensure the stickers are easy to peel and suitable for various surfaces, such as laptops, water bottles, and notebooks.*

5. *Tote Bags:*

- **Material Durability:** *Choose a sturdy canvas or cotton tote bag that can carry everyday items.*
- **Spacious Design:** *Incorporate the podcast logo and key imagery on one side, creating an eye-catching design.*
- **Practicality:** *Consider including a small internal pocket for added functionality.*

6. *Quality Assurance:*

- **Supplier Research:** *Partner with reputable suppliers or manufacturers known for producing high-quality* *merchandise.*

- **Sample Review:** *Personally review sample products to ensure they meet your quality standards. Check for comfort, durability, and accurate representation of the design.*

7. *Sustainability Considerations:*

- **Eco-Friendly Options:** *Explore eco-friendly and sustainable merchandise options, such as organic cotton or recycled materials, aligning with the values of environmentally conscious listeners.*

8. *Accessibility:*

- **Size Range:** *Offer a diverse range of sizes to accommodate various body types and preferences.*
- **International Shipping:** *If your audience is global, choose suppliers that provide reliable international shipping options.*

9. *Pricing Strategy:*

- **Affordability:** *While ensuring quality, aim for a pricing strategy that aligns with your audience's budget.*
- **Bundle Offers:** *Consider creating bundled merchandise packages at a discounted price to encourage multiple purchases.*

10. *Transparent Communication:*

- **Materials and Care Instructions:** *Clearly communicate the materials used in each product and provide care instructions to ensure the longevity of the* *merchandise.*

- **Launch Announcement:** *Excite your audience by announcing the merchandise launch with visuals and descriptions that highlight the quality and appeal of each product.*

By carefully selecting high-quality merchandise that aligns with your audience's preferences, "Adventures Unheard" can provide a tangible and enjoyable extension of the podcast experience, fostering a stronger connection with its dedicated listeners.

5. Partner with a Print-on-Demand Service or Manufacturer: To simplify the logistics of creating and selling merchandise, consider partnering with a print-on-demand service or a manufacturer. These services handle the printing, packaging, and shipping, allowing you to focus on design and promotion. Popular platforms include Printful, Printify, and Merch by Amazon.

Here's a step-by-step guide on how to partner with a print-on-demand service or manufacturer to simplify the logistics of creating and selling merchandise for your podcast:

1. *Research Print-on-Demand Services:*

- Explore popular print-on-demand platforms such as Printful, Printify, and Merch by Amazon.

- Consider factors like product variety, quality, pricing, and user reviews to determine the best fit for your podcast.

2. *Sign Up and Set Up Your Account:*

- Create an account on the chosen print-on-demand platform.

- Complete the necessary setup steps, including providing basic information about your podcast, linking payment details, and configuring your storefront.

3. *Design Your Merchandise:*

- Develop visually appealing designs for your merchandise, incorporating your podcast logo, tagline, or any unique graphics associated with your show.

- Ensure that your designs align with the guidelines and specifications of the print-on-demand service you've chosen.

4. *Select Products and Customize:*

- Browse the product catalog offered by the print-on-demand service.

- Choose the types of merchandise you want to offer, such as T-shirts, hoodies, mugs, stickers, etc.

- Customize each product with your designed graphics, adjusting placement, size, and color as needed.

5. *Set Pricing and Margins:*

- Determine the pricing for each item by considering production costs, platform fees, and desired profit margins.

- Price your merchandise competitively while keeping it appealing to your audience.

6. *Integrate with Your Podcast Platform:*

- If your podcast has a website or an e-commerce platform, integrate the print-on-demand service with your existing setup.

- Utilize any available plugins or APIs to seamlessly sync your merchandise listings with your podcast platform.

7. *Promote Your Merchandise:*

- Start promoting your merchandise through your podcast episodes, social media channels, and other promotional avenues.

- Highlight the unique features of your merchandise, the quality of the products, and any special offers or promotions.

8. *Monitor Sales and Analytics:*

- Regularly check the sales and analytics provided by the print-on-demand platform.

- Use these insights to understand which products are popular, adjust pricing if necessary, and refine your promotional strategies.

9. *Customer Service and Feedback:*

- Be responsive to customer inquiries and feedback related to merchandise.

- Address any issues promptly and use feedback to improve future designs or offerings.

10. *Explore Expansion Opportunities:*

- As your podcast and merchandise gain traction, consider expanding your product offerings or collaborating with influencers to reach a wider audience.

11. *Stay Informed About Platform Updates:*

- Keep yourself updated on any changes or new features introduced by the print-on-demand platform.

- Leverage new tools or options to enhance your merchandise offerings and sales strategy.

By following these steps, you can simplify the logistics of creating and selling merchandise for your podcast, allowing you to focus on what you do best – designing and promoting engaging content.

6. <u>Set Up an Online Store:</u> Create an online store to showcase and sell your podcast merchandise. Platforms like Shopify, Etsy, or Big Cartel provide user-friendly interfaces for setting up an e-commerce store. Customize your store to reflect your podcast's branding.

Creating an online store for your podcast merchandise can be an exciting venture. Here's a step-by-step guide on how to set up an online store using platforms like Shopify, Etsy, or Big Cartel:

1. *Choose Your E-commerce Platform:*

    - **Shopify:** Ideal for a comprehensive and customizable online store experience.

    - **Etsy:** Perfect for creators and artisans, offering a marketplace with built-in traffic.

    - **Big Cartel:** Great for small businesses with a straightforward and easy-to-use interface.

2. *Create an Account:*

    - Sign up for an account on your chosen e-commerce platform.

    - Provide the necessary information to set up your account.

3. *Setup Your Store:*

    - **Shopify:**

        - Follow the onboarding process to set up

your store.

- Choose a unique store name and customize your store settings.

- Add your podcast logo and customize the overall design to align with your branding.

- **Etsy:**

  - Click on "Sell on Etsy" and follow the steps to open your shop.

  - Choose a memorable shop name and fill in your shop preferences.

  - Add a banner and profile picture to make your shop visually appealing.

- **Big Cartel:**

  - Sign in to your account and select "Create a new store."

  - Customize your store settings, including the store name and currency.

  - Add your podcast branding elements, such as a logo and banner.

4. *Add Products:*

- Create product listings for your podcast

merchandise.

- Include high-quality images, detailed descriptions, pricing, and available variations (sizes, colors, etc.).

5. *Customize Your Store:*

- **Shopify:**

    - Explore the theme customization options to match your podcast's branding.

    - Add sections to highlight featured products or promotional content.

- **Etsy:**

    - Customize your shop by selecting a theme that complements your podcast.

    - Add a shop announcement and policies to provide information to your customers.

- **Big Cartel:**

    - Choose a theme that suits your branding and customize it accordingly.

    - Add a header image, customize colors, and set up your store pages.

6. *Set Up Payment and Shipping:*

- Configure payment gateways to receive payments.

- Set up shipping options and provide accurate shipping information.

7. *Launch Your Store:*

- Once everything is set up, review your store to ensure it's ready for launch.

- Announce the opening of your online store through your podcast, social media, and other promotional channels.

8. *Promote Your Store:*

- Utilize your podcast episodes to promote the availability of merchandise.

- Share product listings on social media platforms and engage with your audience.

- Consider running promotions or exclusive discounts to drive initial traffic.

9. *Manage Orders and Customer Service:*

- Keep track of incoming orders through the platform's dashboard.

- Provide excellent customer service by promptly responding to inquiries and processing orders efficiently.

10. *Monitor Analytics:*

- Regularly check the analytics provided by the platform.

- Analyze visitor data, sales performance, and popular products to make informed decisions.

11. *Iterate and Expand:*

- Based on analytics and customer feedback, make necessary adjustments to your store.

- Consider expanding your product line or introducing new merchandise based on demand.

Creating an online store for your podcast merchandise is a fantastic way to engage with your audience and monetize your podcast. Choose the platform that best aligns with your goals and start showcasing your unique creations to the world!

7. <u>Promote Your Merchandise on Your Podcast:</u> Actively promote your merchandise on your podcast episodes. Share the story behind each item, explain its significance, and encourage your audience to support your show by purchasing merchandise. Offer special promotions or discounts for podcast listeners.

Let's explore some examples of how to execute the promotion of your merchandise.

🔦 *Adventures Unheard Merchandise Showcase: Explore the Stories, Wear the Journey!* ✴️

Hello, fellow adventurers! Before we embark on another thrilling episode of "Adventures Unheard," I want to take a moment to share something exciting with you. Our exclusive merchandise line is now available, and each item holds a story as captivating as the tales we uncover in our podcast.

1. The Explorer's T-Shirt:

- *Story:* This isn't just a T-shirt; it's a wearable map of our adventures. The compass rose on the front represents our unwavering curiosity, while the tagline on the back, "Unlock the Tales, Unleash the Unheard," embodies the essence of our podcasting journey.
- *Significance:* By wearing this shirt, you become an honorary explorer, spreading the spirit of discovery wherever you go.

2. Ancient Maps Hoodie:

- *Story:* Picture this: a chilly night by the campfire, surrounded by the mysteries of uncharted lands. That's the inspiration behind our Ancient Maps Hoodie. The design is a tapestry of hidden scrolls and ancient cartography, inviting you to join us in the warmth of storytelling.
- *Significance:* This hoodie wraps you in the magic of our podcast, making every day an adventure.

3. <u>Compass Rose Mug</u>:

- *Story:* Sip your favorite beverage from our Compass Rose Mug and let the spirit of exploration guide your thoughts. The compass rose isn't just a symbol; it's a reminder that every direction holds a story waiting to be heard.
- *Significance:* Your morning coffee becomes a ritual of discovery, awakening your wanderlust.

4. <u>Explorer's Sticker Set</u>:

- *Story:* Our sticker set isn't just a collection of vinyl; it's a gallery of our favorite moments. Each sticker features a variation of our logo, catchphrases, and key imagery. Stick them on your gear, your laptop, or anywhere you want to share the adventure.
- *Significance:* These stickers are like postcards from the places we've explored together, turning your belongings into a canvas of untold stories.

🌟 Special Offer for Podcast Listeners! 🌟

- As a token of our gratitude for your unwavering support, we're offering an exclusive promotion for our podcast listeners. Use the code "ADVENTURE10" at checkout to enjoy a 10% discount on your entire purchase.

How to Get Your Adventure Gear:

Visit our online store at [*AdventuresUnheardMerch.com*]. Explore the stories behind each item and choose your

favorite.
Use the code "ADVENTURE10" at checkout to unlock your exclusive discount.

By purchasing our merchandise, you not only carry a piece of our podcast with you but also contribute to the continued exploration of untold stories.

Thank you for being part of the Adventures Unheard community. Your support fuels our journey, and we can't wait to see you wearing the spirit of adventure!

Happy exploring,

[Your Name]

Host, Adventures Unheard

P.S. Don't forget to share your merch photos with #AdventuresUnheardMerch for a chance to be featured in our upcoming episodes!

8. <u>Utilize Social Media and Your Website:</u> Leverage your podcast's social media accounts and website to promote your merchandise. Share visually appealing images, run giveaways, and create engaging content that highlights your products. Encourage your audience to share photos of themselves with your merchandise.

Leveraging your podcast's social media accounts and website is a powerful way to promote your merchandise. Here's a step-by-step guide on how to effectively do this:

1. *Create Visual Content:*

   - Design visually appealing images featuring your podcast merchandise. Showcase different angles, close-ups, and lifestyle shots.

   - Ensure that the images align with your podcast's branding and capture the essence of your show.

2. *Share Sneak Peeks and Teasers:*

   - Create anticipation by sharing sneak peeks and teasers of upcoming merchandise.

   - Use Instagram Stories, Facebook posts, or Twitter updates to give your audience a behind-the-scenes look at the design process.

3. *Announce Launch on Social Media:*

   - Craft engaging posts to announce the launch of your merchandise on all your social media platforms.

   - Include a call-to-action, inviting followers to explore the collection on your website.

4. *Run Giveaways and Contests:*

   - Host giveaways or contests where followers can win exclusive merchandise.

   - Encourage participants to share your posts, follow your accounts, and tag friends for increased visibility.

5. *Create Engaging Content:*

- Develop engaging content that tells the story behind each merchandise item.

- Share anecdotes, design inspirations, or the significance of specific elements in your products.

6. *Highlight Special Features:*

- Showcase any unique features of your merchandise, such as limited editions, exclusive designs, or special collaborations.

- Emphasize what sets your products apart from others in the market.

7. *Encourage User-Generated Content (UGC):*

- Invite your audience to share photos of themselves with your merchandise.

- Create a branded hashtag (#AdventuresUnheardMerch, for example) and encourages listeners to use it when posting.

8. *Run Limited-Time Promotions:*

- Create a sense of urgency by running limited-time promotions or discounts for your podcast listeners.

- Clearly communicate the promotion period and any special offers on your social media accounts.

9. *Collaborate with Influencers:*

- Partner with influencers or other podcasters in your niche to promote your merchandise.

- Their endorsement can significantly expand your reach and credibility.

10. *Optimize Your Website:*

- Create a dedicated section on your podcast website for merchandise.

- Ensure that the purchasing process is straightforward and user-friendly.

11. *Utilize E-commerce Tools:*

- If you have an online store, use built-in e-commerce tools to integrate product listings directly on your website.

- Ensure that visitors can easily navigate through the merchandise section.

12. *Leverage Podcast Episodes:*

- Mention your merchandise in podcast episodes and provide a direct link to your website.

- Share anecdotes related to specific items to create a deeper connection with your audience.

13. *Engage with Your Audience:*

- Respond to comments and messages on social

media. Engage in conversations about your merchandise.

- Acknowledge and thank listeners who share photos or positive feedback.

14. *Monitor Analytics:*

- Use analytics tools to track engagement, website traffic, and conversions.

- Analyze the performance of different posts and adjust your strategy accordingly.

15. *Consistent Branding Across Platforms:*

- Ensure consistent branding across all social media platforms and your website.

- Use the same logos, colors, and messaging to create a unified brand presence.

16. *Share Testimonials:*

- Feature testimonials or reviews from satisfied customers on your social media accounts and website.

- Real experiences can motivate others to make a purchase.

17. *Newsletter Promotion:*

- Include mentions of your merchandise in your email newsletters.

- Offer exclusive promotions or updates to subscribers to encourage them to visit your online store.

By implementing these strategies, you can create a comprehensive and engaging promotional campaign for your podcast merchandise, fostering a deeper connection with your audience and increasing the visibility of your products.

9. <u>Collaborate with Your Audience:</u> Involve your audience in the creation process by seeking their input on potential designs or merchandise ideas. Consider running design contests or polls to gather feedback. This engagement not only strengthens your community but also ensures that your merchandise resonates with your audience. Here are a few examples that you might consider.

Adventures Unheard Design Quest: Your Voice, Your Merchandise!

Greetings, fellow adventurers! We're embarking on an exciting journey, and this time, we want YOU to be the co-creators of our exclusive merchandise. Your insights and creativity matter, and we can't wait to involve you in every step of the design process.

1. *<u>Design Contest:</u>*

- Share your artistic talents with us! We're hosting a design contest where you can submit your ideas for the next Adventures Unheard merchandise.
- Whether it's a new logo concept, a catchy catchphrase, or an illustration capturing the

spirit of our podcast, we want to see what you envision.

How to Participate:

- Submit your designs by [Date].
- Use the hashtag #AdventuresDesignQuest when sharing on social media.
- The winning design will be featured on a special edition item, and the designer will receive exclusive merchandise and a shoutout on our podcast!

2. *Polls for Product Preferences:*

- We value your opinions! Help us decide which merchandise items to prioritize by participating in polls.
- Head to our Instagram Stories or Twitter polls and vote for your favorite products – T-shirts, hoodies, mugs, stickers, or perhaps something entirely new?

How to Vote:

- Keep an eye on our social media for polls.
- Cast your votes and let your preferences shape our merchandise collection.

3. *Theme Suggestions:*

- Your creativity inspires us! Share your theme suggestions for upcoming merchandise collections.

- Whether it's a specific adventure theme, a historical era, or a nod to a memorable podcast episode, your ideas could be the guiding force behind our next design concept.

How to Share Your Themes:

- Drop your suggestions in the comments on our social media posts.
- Feel free to explain the significance behind your theme ideas.

4. *Live Design Q&A:*

- Let's chat in real-time! Join us for a live design Q&A session where we discuss potential designs, themes, and merchandise ideas.
- Your questions, feedback, and suggestions will be the heartbeat of this interactive session.

How to Participate:

- Stay tuned for announcements about the live session on [Date].
- Bring your questions, suggestions, and enthusiasm!

Why Get Involved?

- Community Spirit: This is your chance to actively contribute to the Adventures Unheard community.

- Exclusive Access: Participants will get a sneak peek into the design process and be the first to know about upcoming merchandise launches.
- Recognition: Your name could be featured in podcast episodes, social media shoutouts, or even on the tags of our exclusive merchandise.

Our podcast is not just about storytelling; it's about creating a shared adventure. Join us in shaping the visual narrative of Adventures Unheard!

Happy designing,

[Your Name]

Host, Adventures Unheard

P.S. Ready to embark on this design quest together? Share your creativity with us, and let's make our merchandise as extraordinary as our podcast! 🚀 #AdventuresDesignQuest

10. Offer Bundle Deals or Limited-Time Offers: Boost sales by offering bundle deals or limited-time promotions. For example, you could create bundles that include multiple items at a discounted price or run special promotions during specific events or milestones for your podcast. Here are a few ways to do it.

🌟 Adventures Unheard Exclusive Bundles & Promotions: Elevate Your Adventure Collection! 🎒

Greetings, fellow explorers! We've got thrilling news that will add a spark to your journey with

Adventures Unheard. To make your merchandise experience even more exciting, we're introducing exclusive bundle deals and limited-time promotions that you won't want to miss!

1. _Adventure Essentials Bundle:_

- ⬤ Unleash the full adventure experience with our Adventure Essentials Bundle!
- 🎒 Includes the iconic Explorer's T-Shirt, Ancient Maps Hoodie, and the must-have Compass Rose Mug.
- 🪁 Limited-time Offer: Get all three for the special price of $X (Original Price: $Y).

2. _Podcast Power Pack:_

- 🎧 Elevate your podcast listening with our Podcast Power Pack!
- 🚀 Includes an Adventures Unheard T-Shirt, a set of Explorer's Stickers, and an exclusive podcast-themed Tote Bag.
- 🪁 Bundle Deal: Dive into the Power Pack for only $Z (Original Price: $W).

3. _Explorer's Combo:_

- ✨ Mix and match your favorite items with our Explorer's Combo!
- 🛒 Choose any two merchandise items and enjoy a combo discount.
- 🪁 Limited-time Offer: Create your combo for $A (Original Price: $B).

4. *Special Milestone Celebration:*

- 🎉 As we reach [Podcast Milestone], join the celebration with special promotions!
- 🛍️ Enjoy a [X]% discount on all merchandise for the next [Y] days.
- 🎊 Use code "MILESTONE[X]" at checkout to unlock your exclusive savings.

How to Get Your Exclusive Adventure Bundles:

Visit our online store at [AdventuresUnheardMerch.com].
Explore the exclusive bundles and promotions section.
Add your favorite bundles to your cart and use the designated codes during checkout to unlock the special prices.

Why Dive into these Deals?

- 🏷️ Save Big: Enjoy significant savings on high-quality merchandise.
- 🛍️ Exclusive Items: Some bundles include items available only in these limited-time offers.
- 🚀 Support the Adventure: Your purchase fuels our podcasting journey and unlocks more thrilling stories.

Act Fast – Limited Quantities Available!

These bundles and promotions are available for a limited time only, and quantities are limited. Grab your adventure essentials before they're gone!

Embark on this exciting merch journey with Adventures Unheard. Your support is the compass guiding us through uncharted territories!

Happy shopping,

[Your Name]

Host, Adventures Unheard

P.S. Don't forget to share your bundled adventures using #AdventuresUnheardBundles! ▟

11. Ensure Seamless Fulfillment and Customer Service: Partner with reliable fulfillment services to ensure that orders are processed efficiently, and customers receive their merchandise in a timely manner. Provide excellent customer service by addressing inquiries promptly and addressing any issues that may arise.

Partnering with reliable fulfillment services is crucial to ensuring a smooth and efficient process for processing orders and delivering merchandise to your customers. *Here's a step-by-step guide on how to establish and maintain a successful partnership:*

1. *Research and Choose Fulfillment Services:*

   - Identify reputable fulfillment services that align with the needs and scale of your podcast merchandise.

   - Consider factors such as shipping capabilities, order processing speed, customer reviews, and

integration options with your chosen
e-commerce platform.

2. *Create Accounts and Set Up Integration:*

- Sign up for an account with the chosen
  fulfillment service.

- Integrate the fulfillment service with your online
  store or e-commerce platform to automate
  order processing.

3. *Provide Detailed Product Information:*

- Ensure that your product listings on the
  fulfillment service platform include accurate and
  detailed information.

- Specify product dimensions, weights, and any
  special handling instructions.

4. *Test the Integration:*

- Conduct test orders to verify that the integration
  between your online store and the fulfillment
  service is seamless.

- Confirm that order details, including product
  variants and quantities, are accurately
  transmitted.

5. *Set Clear Expectations:*

- Clearly communicate your expectations
  regarding processing times, shipping methods,

and any other relevant information to the fulfillment service.

- Discuss service level agreements (SLAs) and confirm that they align with your customers' expectations.

6. *Monitor Inventory Levels:*

- Keep track of your merchandise inventory with the fulfillment service.

- Set up alerts or notifications for low stock levels to avoid backorders.

7. *Address Customer Inquiries Promptly:*

- Provide excellent customer service by promptly responding to customer inquiries about orders and shipping.

- Ensure that your customer support team is well-informed about the fulfillment process.

8. *Implement Order Tracking:*

- Enable order tracking so that customers can monitor the status of their shipments in real-time.

- Communicate tracking information to customers as soon as orders are fulfilled.

9. *Handle Returns Efficiently:*

- Establish a process for handling returns in collaboration with the fulfillment service.

- Clearly communicate your return policy to customers and provide instructions for returning merchandise.

10. *Regularly Review Performance:*

- Regularly assess the performance of the fulfillment service.

- Monitor order processing times, shipping accuracy, and customer satisfaction to identify areas for improvement.

11. *Address Issues Promptly:*

- If issues arise, such as delays or errors in order processing, address them promptly and communicate transparently with affected customers.

- Work closely with the fulfillment service to implement corrective measures.

12. *Seek Customer Feedback:*

- Encourage customers to provide feedback on their overall shopping and shipping experience.

- Use feedback to make informed decisions and enhance the customer experience.

13. *Review Fulfillment Service Performance:*

- Periodically review the performance of the fulfillment service based on key metrics and customer feedback.

- Consider exploring alternative services or making adjustments if necessary.

14. *Maintain Open Communication:*

- Foster a relationship with the fulfillment service through open and transparent communication.

- Keep them informed about any changes in your merchandise, promotions, or anticipated order volumes.

15. *Explore Additional Services:*

- As your podcast and merchandise grow, explore additional services offered by fulfillment partners, such as international shipping options, personalized packaging, or branded inserts.

By following these steps and maintaining a collaborative and communicative relationship with your chosen fulfillment service, you can ensure that your podcast merchandise orders are processed efficiently and that customers receive their items in a timely and satisfactory manner. This approach contributes significantly to a positive customer experience and enhances the overall success of your podcast merchandise venture.

12. Collect and Showcase Customer Reviews: Encourage

customers to leave reviews for your merchandise. Positive reviews build trust and can influence potential buyers. Showcase these reviews on your website and social media platforms to highlight the satisfaction of your customers.

Encouraging customers to leave reviews for your merchandise is a powerful way to build trust and influence potential buyers. Here's a comprehensive guide on how to prompt reviews, showcase them effectively, and leverage positive feedback on your website and social media platforms:

1. *Provide an Exceptional Customer Experience:*

   - Ensure that the overall shopping experience, from browsing your online store to receiving the merchandise, is exceptional.

   - Customers are more likely to leave positive reviews when they have a positive overall experience.

2. *Send Follow-Up Emails:*

   - After a customer has received their merchandise, send a follow-up email thanking them for their purchase.

   - Include a friendly request to leave a review and provide a direct link to the review platform on your website.

3. *Incorporate Review Requests in Packaging:*

   - Include a small note or card within the

packaging encouraging customers to share their thoughts.

- Mention that their feedback is valued and can help enhance the shopping experience for others.

4. *Create a Seamless Review Process:*

- Ensure that leaving a review is a straightforward process. Include clear instructions and minimize the number of steps required.

- Consider integrating review options directly into your website or using popular review platforms.

5. *Offer Incentives:*

- Consider offering a small incentive for leaving a review, such as a discount on their next purchase.

- Make sure that incentives comply with the policies of the review platforms you use.

6. *Highlight the Importance of Feedback:*

- Communicate to your customers that their feedback is valuable and plays a crucial role in improving your products and services.

- Emphasize that their reviews contribute to the growth of your podcast and merchandise.

7. *Timing Matters:*

- Choose the right time to request a review. Sending the request shortly after the customer has received the merchandise allows their experience to be fresh in their minds.

8. *Engage with Existing Reviews:*

- Respond to existing reviews, whether positive or negative, to show that you value customer feedback.

- Engaging with reviews creates a sense of community and encourages others to share their experiences.

9. *Showcase Reviews on Your Website:*

- Create a dedicated section on your website to display customer reviews.

- Include a mix of positive reviews that highlight different aspects of your merchandise and service.

10. *Integrate Reviews into Product Pages:*

- Display customer reviews directly on your product pages to influence potential buyers.

- Many e-commerce platforms have plugins or built-in features for showcasing reviews.

11. *Utilize Social Media Platforms:*

- Share snippets of positive reviews on your social media channels.

- Create visually appealing graphics featuring customer quotes and use them in your social media posts.

12. *Create Review Highlights:*

- Periodically create highlight posts featuring several positive reviews.

- Use engaging visuals and include a call-to-action encouraging others to share their experiences.

13. *Run Review Campaigns:*

- Launch review campaigns on social media, encouraging followers to share their thoughts.

- Use specific hashtags related to your podcast or merchandise to aggregate reviews.

14. *Host a Review Contest:*

- Host a contest where customers can enter by leaving a review.

- Offer attractive prizes or exclusive merchandise as incentives.

15. *Express Gratitude:*

- Publicly thank customers who leave positive

reviews on social media.

- Showcasing appreciation encourages more customers to share their experiences.

16. *Share User-Generated Content:*

- If customers share photos of themselves with your merchandise, feature these images along with their reviews.

- User-generated content adds authenticity and resonates with potential buyers.

17. *Monitor and Respond:*

- Regularly monitor review platforms and respond to new reviews.

- Acknowledge positive reviews and address any concerns raised in negative reviews.

18. *Implement Feedback:*

- Act on constructive feedback received in reviews to improve your merchandise and overall customer experience.

- Communicate to your audience how their feedback has led to positive changes.

Creating a culture of feedback and showcase the satisfaction of your customers, enhancing trust and credibility for your podcast merchandise. Positive reviews not only influence potential buyers but also contribute to the growth and success of your podcasting venture.

By following these steps, you can create and sell branded merchandise related to your podcast, turning your show into a tangible and meaningful part of your audience's lives.

CHAPTER 6

Premium Content

Offering premium or exclusive content to subscribers who pay a monthly fee is a compelling way to monetize your podcast and provide added value to your most dedicated audience. Here's how to implement this strategy effectively:

1. **<u>Choose a Platform for Exclusive Content:</u>** Select a platform that supports premium or exclusive content for your subscribers. Platforms like Patreon, Supercast, or your podcast hosting provider may offer features to set up subscription tiers and deliver exclusive content.

Selecting the right platform to support premium or exclusive content for your subscribers is crucial for the success of your subscription-based model. Here's a step-by-step guide on how to choose and utilize a platform that offers features to set up subscription tiers and deliver exclusive content:

1. *<u>Identify Your Content Goals:</u>*

   - Define the type of premium or exclusive content you plan to offer.

   - Consider whether you'll provide early access to episodes, bonus episodes, behind-the-scenes content, exclusive interviews, or other special perks.

2. _Research Subscription Platforms:_

- Explore popular subscription platforms such as Patreon, Supercast, and other podcast hosting providers that offer subscription features.

- Look for platforms that align with your content goals, audience size, and budget.

3. _Evaluate Platform Features:_

- Compare the features offered by different subscription platforms.

- Check if they support multiple subscription tiers, allow you to set pricing, offer easy payment processing, and provide tools for content delivery.

4. _Consider Integration with Your Podcast Hosting:_

- If possible, choose a platform that seamlessly integrates with your podcast hosting provider.

- Integration simplifies the process of uploading and delivering exclusive content to subscribers.

5. _Examine Pricing and Fees:_

- Review the pricing structure and any fees associated with using the platform.

- Consider how pricing aligns with your budget and whether the platform offers value for the features provided.

6. *Understand Payment Processing:*

- Ensure that the platform provides secure and reliable payment processing.

- Familiarize yourself with how payments are processed, the frequency of payouts, and any transaction fees.

7. *Explore Subscription Tiers:*

- Look for platforms that allow you to set up multiple subscription tiers.

- Each tier can offer different benefits or levels of exclusive content to cater to various subscriber preferences.

8. *Customize Subscription Plans:*

- Choose a platform that allows customization of subscription plans, including naming tiers, setting pricing, and outlining benefits.

- Tailor plans to provide a compelling value proposition for subscribers.

9. *Create Compelling Benefits:*

- Determine the exclusive benefits subscribers will receive at each tier.

- Craft compelling descriptions for each tier, clearly outlining what subscribers can expect.

10. *Promote Your Subscription Model:*

- Once set up, actively promote your subscription model through your podcast episodes, social media, and other promotional channels.

- Clearly communicate the value of subscribing and the exclusive content available.

11. *Deliver Exclusive Content:*

- Regularly create and upload exclusive content for your subscribers.

- Utilize the platform's tools to schedule releases and control access based on subscription tiers.

12. Engage with Your Subscribers:

- Foster a sense of community by engaging with your subscribers through comments, Q&A sessions, or exclusive live events.

- Make them feel valued for their support.

13. *Monitor Analytics:*

- Use the analytics provided by the platform to track subscriber growth, engagement, and revenue.

- Analyze which content resonates most with your audience.

14. *Iterate Based on Feedback:*

    - Collect feedback from your subscribers and iterate on your subscription model.

    - Consider introducing new benefits or adjusting pricing tiers based on audience preferences.

15. *Stay Compliant with Terms of Service:*

    - Familiarize yourself with the terms of service of the chosen platform.

    - Ensure that your content and promotional strategies comply with their guidelines.

16. *Communicate Changes to Subscribers:*

    - Transparently communicate any changes to subscription plans or exclusive content to your subscribers.

    - Keep them informed about upcoming benefits and events.

17. *Stay Informed about Platform Updates:*

    - Stay informed about updates and new features rolled out by the platform.

    - Take advantage of new tools that enhance your ability to deliver premium content.

Choosing the right platform and effectively implementing a subscription model for premium or exclusive content requires careful consideration. By selecting a platform that aligns with your goals and audience preferences, you can create a successful subscription-based offering for your podcast.

2. **<u>Define Subscription Tiers:</u>** Establish different subscription tiers with varying levels of benefits. For example, you could have a basic tier with access to exclusive episodes and a higher tier with additional perks like behind-the-scenes content, Q&A sessions, or merchandise discounts.

Here's an example of establishing different subscription tiers for a podcast:

Tier 1: Basic Listener

- Monthly Fee: $5

- Benefits:

  - Access to exclusive monthly episodes.

  - Early access to regular podcast episodes.

  - Participation in community polls to influence content.

Tier 2: Superfan Supporter

- Monthly Fee: $10

- Benefits:

  - All benefits from Tier 1.

  - Exclusive behind-the-scenes content,

including bloopers and outtakes.

- Personalized shoutouts in select episodes.

- Access to a private community forum for discussions.

Tier 3: VIP Insider

- Monthly Fee: $20

- Benefits:

  - All benefits from Tiers 1 and 2.

  - Monthly Q&A sessions with the podcast hosts.

  - Early access to event tickets and live show recordings.

  - Digital download of podcast transcripts.

Tier 4: Premium Patron

- Monthly Fee: $50

- Benefits:

  - All benefits from Tiers 1, 2, and 3.

  - Exclusive merchandise discounts (20% off on all podcast merchandise).

- Limited edition podcast merchandise shipped quarterly.

- Priority consideration for submitted listener questions in Q&A sessions.

Tier 5: Ultimate Insider

- Monthly Fee: $100

- Benefits:

  - All benefits from Tiers 1, 2, 3, and 4.

  - Quarterly personalized voice messages from the hosts.

  - Exclusive access to live virtual events with the hosts.

  - Annual one-on-one video call with a host for personalized podcast recommendations and discussions.

This tiered subscription model allows listeners to choose a level that aligns with their budget and desired level of engagement. The progression of benefits creates a sense of exclusivity and appreciation for supporters at each tier, encouraging listeners to consider higher levels for additional perks.

3. Create Compelling Exclusive Content: Develop exclusive content that is highly engaging and distinct from your regular episodes. This could include bonus episodes, in-depth interviews, early access to content, or specialized series that cater to the interests of your premium subscribers.

Developing exclusive content that is highly engaging and distinct from regular episodes involves a thoughtful strategy to cater to the interests of premium subscribers. Here's a step-by-step guide on how to achieve this:

Understand Your Audience:
- Conduct surveys, polls, or gather feedback to understand the specific interests and preferences of your audience. This insight will help you tailor exclusive content that resonates with them.

Identify Premium Subscriber Interests:
- Analyze the data from your existing audience to identify common themes or topics that resonate well. Use this information to tailor exclusive content that aligns with these interests.

Plan Bonus Episodes:
- Create bonus episodes that go beyond the regular content. This could include behind-the scenes looks, personal reflections, or explorations of topics in greater detail. Ensure that the bonus content feels exclusive and valuable.

Conduct In-Depth Interviews:
- Reach out to industry experts, thought leaders, or individuals with unique perspectives related to your podcast theme. Schedule exclusive interviews that delve deep into their experiences and insights.

Offer Early Access:
- Provide premium subscribers with early access to regular episodes. This not only makes them

feel special but also creates a sense of exclusivity, as they get to enjoy the content before the general audience.

Create Specialized Series:

- Develop specialized series that cater to specific niche interests within your podcast theme. This could be a mini-series exploring a particular aspect or theme in more detail, offering a more immersive experience for premium subscribers.

Interactive Content:

- Engage premium subscribers through live Q&A sessions, webinars, or virtual events. Allow them to actively participate, ask questions, and provide feedback, creating a more personalized connection.

Exclusive Resources:

- Provide premium subscribers with downloadable resources such as guides, checklists, or e-books related to the content covered in your podcast. This adds tangible value to their subscription.

Member-Only Community:

- Establish a private community or forum exclusively for premium subscribers. Foster discussions, allow them to connect with each other, and provide direct access to you for a more personalized experience.

Personalized Shoutouts and Recognition:

- Acknowledge and appreciate your premium subscribers in your regular episodes. Offer personalized shoutouts, express gratitude, and make them feel recognized for their support.

Consistent Schedule:

- Maintain a consistent schedule for releasing exclusive content. Whether it's monthly bonus episodes, weekly live sessions, or periodic specialized series, consistency is key to keeping premium subscribers engaged.

Collect and Analyze Feedback:
- Actively seek feedback from premium subscribers. Use surveys, social media, or direct communication to understand what they enjoy, what they want more of, and how you can further enhance their experience.

By incorporating these strategies, you can develop exclusive content that not only meets the expectations of your premium subscribers but also adds significant value to their subscription, fostering a loyal and engaged audience.

4. <u>Promote Exclusive Content Regularly:</u> Actively promote your exclusive content across your podcast episodes, social media channels, and email newsletters. Remind your audience about the additional value they can access by becoming premium subscribers.

Promoting your exclusive content effectively is crucial to encourage your audience to become premium subscribers. Here's a guide on how to actively promote your exclusive content across different channels:

Incorporate Call-to-Actions in Regular Episodes:
- Include promotional messages and call-to-actions within your regular episodes, encouraging listeners to become premium subscribers to access exclusive content. Mention the additional value they can unlock by subscribing.
-

Tease Exclusive Content in Regular Episodes:
- Provide teasers or highlights of exclusive content during regular episodes. Create intrigue and excitement, making listeners curious about what they could access as premium subscribers.

Dedicated Promo Segments:
- Designate specific segments within your regular episodes to promote premium content. Share snippets, anecdotes, or behind-the-scenes insights to entice listeners to subscribe for the full experience.

Consistent Messaging Across Platforms:
- Ensure a cohesive message across all your platforms. Use consistent branding and messaging when promoting exclusive content on your podcast, social media, and newsletters to reinforce the value of premium subscriptions.

Leverage Social Media:
- Regularly share posts on your social media channels highlighting exclusive content. Create visually appealing graphics, teaser videos, or engaging captions to capture attention. Use relevant hashtags to increase discoverability.

Live Announcements:
- Use live sessions on platforms like Instagram, Facebook, or Twitter to make real-time announcements about exclusive content. Answer questions, address concerns, and generate excitement during these live sessions.

Create Countdowns:
- Build anticipation by creating countdowns for the release of exclusive content. Use countdown graphics, stories, or posts on social media to remind your audience about upcoming premium releases.

Email Newsletters:
- Include dedicated sections in your regular email newsletters promoting exclusive content. Craft compelling subject lines and provide direct links for easy access to premium subscription details.

Offer Limited-Time Promotions:
- Create a sense of urgency by occasionally offering limited-time promotions or discounts for premium subscriptions. Highlight these promotions across all channels to encourage immediate action.

User Testimonials:
- Share testimonials from current premium subscribers. Highlight their positive experiences and the value they've gained from exclusive content. This social proof can be a powerful motivator for potential subscribers.

Collaborate with Influencers:
- Partner with influencers or thought leaders in your niche to promote your premium content. Their endorsement can lend credibility and introduce your exclusive offerings to a wider audience.

Engage with Listener Feedback:
- Actively engage with listener feedback and incorporate suggestions into your promotions. Show that you value their opinions and are committed to delivering content that resonates with them.

Create Highlight Reels:
- Compile highlight reels or compilations from your exclusive content. Share these reels on social media or in regular episodes to showcase the quality and uniqueness of premium content.

Offer Free Trials:

- Consider offering free trials for premium subscriptions. Allow listeners to experience the exclusive content for a limited period before committing to a subscription, enticing them to explore the additional value.

By implementing these strategies consistently, you can effectively promote your exclusive content across multiple channels, maximizing visibility and encouraging more listeners to become premium subscribers.

5. <u>Offer Early Access to Episodes:</u> Provide premium subscribers with early access to your regular episodes. This can be a strong incentive for listeners who want to stay ahead of the curve and be the first to enjoy your content. Here are some ways to do it.

🔒 TechInsights Premium Early Access: Be the First to Unleash the Future! 🚀

Dear TechInsights Community,

Exciting news! We're thrilled to introduce TechInsights Premium Early Access — an exclusive opportunity for our dedicated supporters to stay at the forefront of the tech world.

🎧 What's Early Access?

Starting this week, TechInsights Premium subscribers get a 48-hour head start on our regular episodes. While the world awaits, you get to dive into the most cutting-edge tech insights before anyone else.

🌐 Why Early Access?

Tech moves at lightning speed, and we know you want to be in the know, stay ahead of the curve, and be the first to share the latest breakthroughs with your peers.

🚀 How It Works:

> *Become a TechInsights Premium Subscriber: Visit [Link to Subscribe] to unlock the Early Access perk.*
> *Get Notified: As a Premium member, you'll receive an exclusive notification 48 hours before the official episode release.*
> *Enjoy the Future of Tech: Access the episode before it goes live for the general audience and be the trendsetter in your tech circles.*

✴ Exclusive Bonus:

Alongside early access, TechInsights Premium subscribers will also receive occasional bonus content, extended interviews, and insider updates to elevate your tech experience.

🎤 Join the Inner Circle:

TechInsights Premium isn't just about early access; it's about community and connection. Join our private forums, engage in discussions, and shape the future of the podcast with your insights.

Ready to be a tech trailblazer? Subscribe to TechInsights Premium now and unlock a new era of tech exploration!

[Subscribe Now]

Thank you for being part of the TechInsights family. Together, let's explore the future, today!

Best,

[Your Podcast Host]

This example creates a sense of exclusivity, emphasizes the importance of staying ahead in the tech world, and provides a clear call-to-action for interested listeners to become premium subscribers.

6. <u>Host Live Events or Q&A Sessions:</u> Arrange live events or Q&A sessions exclusively for premium subscribers. This interactive experience allows you to connect directly with your most dedicated audience, answering their questions and providing a more personalized experience.

Arranging live events or Q&A sessions exclusively for premium subscribers is a great way to foster a sense of community and provide a more personalized experience. Here's a guide on how to organize such interactive sessions:

Choose the Right Platform:
- Select a platform that facilitates live interactions, such as Zoom, Facebook Live, YouTube Live, or Instagram Live. Consider the preferences of your audience and the features offered by each platform.

Schedule Regular Sessions:
- Establish a consistent schedule for live events or Q&A sessions. This could be a monthly or bi-monthly occurrence to keep your premium subscribers engaged and looking forward to the interactive sessions.

Announce Sessions in Advance:
- Clearly communicate the schedule of upcoming live events or Q&A sessions well in advance. Use your podcast episodes, social media, and newsletters to announce the dates and encourage participation.

Create Exclusive Invitations:
- Send exclusive invitations or access links to your premium subscribers via email or through a dedicated communication channel. This reinforces the exclusivity of the event and makes subscribers feel valued.

Encourage Questions in Advance:
- Invite premium subscribers to submit questions in advance. This allows you to prepare thoughtful responses and ensures that the session covers topics of interest to your dedicated audience.

Use Branded Graphics and Promotion:
- Create branded graphics and promotional materials to highlight the upcoming live event or Q&A session. Consistent branding reinforces the connection between the event and your podcast.

Moderate Effectively:
- Designate a moderator to facilitate the session and manage the flow of questions. This person can ensure that the session stays on track, all relevant questions are addressed, and the atmosphere remains engaging.

Interact in Real-Time:
- During the live event, actively engage with your premium subscribers in real-time. Respond to questions, acknowledge comments, and create a conversational atmosphere. This direct

interaction strengthens the bond between you and your audience.

Record and Share:

- Record the live events or Q&A sessions and make them available exclusively to premium subscribers who couldn't attend. This provides additional value and allows all premium members to access the content.

Collect Feedback:

- Encourage feedback after each live event. Use surveys, polls, or direct messages to understand what worked well, what could be improved, and what topics your audience would like to explore in future sessions.

Offer Exclusive Insights:

- Provide exclusive insights or behind-the-scenes information during the live events. This could include sneak peeks into upcoming episodes, special announcements, or exclusive content previews for premium subscribers.

Promote Community Interaction:

- Foster community interaction among premium subscribers during the live events. Encourage them to share their thoughts, experiences, and tips with each other, creating a supportive and engaging atmosphere.

By following these steps, you can effectively organize live events or Q&A sessions exclusively for your premium subscribers, creating a unique and interactive experience that strengthens your relationship with your most dedicated audience.

7. <u>Include Personalized Shout-Outs:</u> Give personalized shout-outs or thank-you messages to premium subscribers in your episodes. Acknowledging their support adds a personal touch and makes them feel valued as integral members of your podcast community.

Let's consider an example for a podcast named "Adventurous Ears," which explores travel, adventure, and storytelling. In this example, the host gives personalized shout-outs to premium subscribers:

● Adventurous Ears: A Heartfelt Thank-You to Our Journey Companions! ▮

Greetings, fellow adventurers of Adventurous Ears! Before we embark on another expedition through the tales of the world, I want to express profound gratitude to the spirited souls who make our podcast possible — our incredible Premium Subscribers!

✺ A Shout-out to [Subscriber Name 1]:

"A hearty shout-out to [Subscriber Name 1], an intrepid explorer in our community! Your support fuels the wanderlust at the core of our podcast. May your adventures be filled with fascinating stories and discoveries in every corner of the globe."

◆ Cheers to [Subscriber Name 2]:

"Sending enthusiastic cheers and sincere thanks to [Subscriber Name 2] for being a steadfast supporter of our storytelling escapades. Your dedication to embracing the spirit of adventure is truly commendable. May your journey be adorned with thrilling narratives and unexpected twists."

■ Special Appreciation for [Subscriber Name 3]:

"A special note of appreciation to [Subscriber Name 3] for infusing our adventures with your unique energy. Your commitment to exploring the world through the power of stories is a guiding light. May your travels be filled with diverse cultures and unforgettable experiences."

To all our Premium Subscribers, you are the compass guiding us through the narratives of Adventurous Ears. Your dedication to the spirit of exploration shapes our podcast's journey.

If you haven't joined our adventurous community yet, consider becoming a Premium Subscriber at our expedition hub. Unlock exclusive content and become an integral part of our journey into the captivating world of adventure storytelling.

Thank you for being the journey companions of Adventurous Ears. Now, let's set sail into another episode and continue our exploration of the vast and wondrous stories together!

With adventurous gratitude,

[Your Podcast Explorer]

This example creates an adventurous and appreciative atmosphere, emphasizing the community's commitment to exploring the world through stories. It adds a personal touch, making subscribers feel valued and recognized for their contributions to the podcast's exploration of adventure and storytelling.

8. <u>Provide Exclusive Merchandise:</u> Include exclusive merchandise as part of premium subscription packages. Branded items, such as T-shirts, stickers, or mugs, create a sense of exclusivity and tangible rewards for subscribers.

Let's create an example for a podcast called "Adventure Seekers Unleashed," which focuses on travel, exploration, and outdoor adventures. In this example, the podcast offers exclusive merchandise as part of its premium subscription packages:

● Adventure Seekers Unleashed Premium Club: Your Passport to Exclusive Merchandise! ■

Embark on a journey like never before with Adventure Seekers Unleashed Premium Club! As a token of our appreciation for your adventurous spirit, we're thrilled to introduce exclusive branded merchandise that will accompany you on your wildest escapades.

Premium Subscription Tiers:

Explorer Tier - $5/month:
- Exclusive Sticker Pack:
  - Dive into the adventure with a set of high-quality, weather-resistant stickers featuring our podcast logo and iconic travel symbols.

Adventurer Tier - $10/month:
- Adventure Seekers Unleashed T-shirt:
  - Wear your passion proudly with a custom-designed T-shirt that showcases your love for exploration and adventure.

Trailblazer Tier - $20/month:
- Explorer Kit:
  - Receive a premium-quality Adventure Seekers Unleashed T-shirt and an exclusive enamel mug – perfect for

sipping your favorite beverage by the campfire.

What Makes Our Merchandise Special?

- Limited Edition: *All merchandise items are exclusive to Premium Club members and won't be available anywhere else.*
- High-Quality Materials: *Our T-shirts are made from soft, breathable cotton, stickers are weather-resistant, and mugs are durable enamel – designed to withstand your adventurous lifestyle.*
- Global Design Influence: *The designs are inspired by the diverse cultures and landscapes encountered during our podcast journeys.*

How to Join the Adventure Seekers Unleashed Premium Club?

Visit our website: *Premium Club*
Choose your preferred subscription tier.
Dive into exclusive content, early access, and receive your Adventure Seekers Unleashed merchandise at your doorstep.

Unleash the Adventure, Become a Premium Explorer Today!

Join our community of adventure enthusiasts, gain access to premium content, and carry a piece of Adventure Seekers Unleashed with you on every expedition. Your subscription not only unlocks thrilling experiences but also supports the production of more exciting content.

Ready to explore? Join the Adventure Seekers Unleashed Premium Club and let the adventures begin!

This example creates a clear structure for different subscription tiers, highlights the uniqueness of the merchandise, and emphasizes the value of being part of the Premium Club. It encourages potential subscribers to join and become a part of the exclusive adventure community.

9. <u>Foster Community Interaction:</u> Encourage interaction among premium subscribers by creating a dedicated community or forum. This allows them to connect with each other, discuss exclusive content, and share their experiences as part of the premium subscription community.

Encouraging interaction among premium subscribers through a dedicated community or forum is a great way to foster a sense of belonging and enhance the overall subscription experience. Here's a step-by-step guide on how to create and promote such a community:

Step 1: Choose a Platform

Select a Community Platform:

- Choose a platform that suits your audience and the type of interactions you want to facilitate. Options include forums, social media groups, or even a dedicated section on your website.

Step 2: Set Up the Community

Create a Dedicated Section:

- If using an existing platform, create a dedicated section specifically for premium subscribers. If setting up a new community, design it with user-friendly features and clear categories.

Establish Community Guidelines:

- Clearly outline community guidelines to ensure a positive and respectful environment. Emphasize the importance of constructive discussions and adherence to the community's purpose.

Step 3: Integrate Exclusive Content

Exclusive Content Section:

- Include a section where premium subscribers can discuss and share thoughts about exclusive content. This could include episodes, early releases, or behind-the-scenes insights.

Step 4: Promote the Community

Announce the Community:

- Promote the launch of the community through various channels, including podcast episodes, social media, and email newsletters. Clearly communicate the benefits of joining.

Incentivize Participation:

- Encourage participation by highlighting exclusive perks for community members. This could include Q&A sessions with hosts, exclusive content previews, or even occasional giveaways.

Step 5: Facilitate Engagement

Pose Discussion Starters:

- Regularly post discussion starters related to podcast episodes or broader topics within the community. This encourages members to share their thoughts and experiences.

Host Live Sessions:

- Schedule live Q&A sessions or discussions with hosts. This real-time interaction creates a dynamic community atmosphere.

Step 6: Acknowledge and Appreciate

Highlight Member Contributions:

- Acknowledge and celebrate valuable contributions from community members. This can be through shout-outs in podcast episodes, social media mentions, or dedicated community posts.

Host Virtual Events:

- Organize virtual events exclusive to the community, such as webinars, virtual meet-ups, or themed discussions. This fosters a stronger sense of connection.

Step 7: Gather Feedback and Iterate

Seek Feedback:

- Regularly seek feedback from community members about their experience. Use surveys or discussion threads to gather insights on how to improve and tailor the community to their needs.

Iterate and Improve:

- Implement changes based on feedback to continuously improve the community. This might involve refining guidelines, introducing new discussion topics, or enhancing community features.

Step 8: Keep the Momentum

Consistent Engagement:

- Maintain a consistent presence in the community. Regularly engage with members, respond to discussions, and keep the energy alive.

Promote Community Events:

- Continuously promote upcoming events, discussions, or exclusive content releases to keep members excited and active.

By following these steps, you can create a vibrant and engaging premium subscriber community, enhancing the overall experience for your dedicated audience.

10. <u>Regularly Evaluate and Update Offerings:</u> Periodically evaluate the performance of your premium offerings and gather feedback from subscribers. Use this information to refine your content strategy, introduce new perks, or adjust subscription tiers based on the evolving needs and preferences of your audience.

Periodically evaluating the performance of your premium offerings and gathering feedback from subscribers is crucial for maintaining a successful and dynamic subscription model. Here's a step-by-step guide on how to effectively assess and improve your premium offerings:

<u>Step 1: Set Evaluation Periods</u>

Establish Evaluation Cycles:

- Define specific time intervals (e.g., quarterly or bi-annually) to assess the performance of your premium offerings. This ensures regular feedback and adaptation to changing audience preferences.

<u>Step 2: Utilize Analytics</u>

Analyze Subscriber Data:

- Utilize analytics tools to track subscriber engagement, retention rates, and consumption patterns. Evaluate which premium content performs well and identify any areas for improvement.

Track Subscriber Growth:

- Monitor the growth or contraction of your premium subscriber base over time. Identify trends and patterns related to promotions, content releases, or external factors.

Step 3: Gather Direct Feedback

Conduct Surveys:

- Periodically send surveys to your premium subscribers to gather direct feedback. Ask about their favorite content, areas for improvement, and suggestions for new perks or features.

Host Q&A Sessions:

- Arrange live Q&A sessions or virtual meetings with your premium subscribers. This direct interaction allows you to understand their needs and preferences in real-time.

Step 4: Review Content Performance

Analyze Content Metrics:

- Dive into specific metrics related to premium content, such as episode downloads, watch times, or participation rates in exclusive events. Identify the most popular and least engaging content.

Step 5: Assess Subscriber Engagement

Evaluate Community Engagement:

- If you have a premium community or forum, assess member participation. Track discussions, comments, and overall engagement to understand the community dynamics.

Monitor Social Media:

- Keep an eye on social media platforms for mentions, comments, and discussions related to your premium offerings. This external feedback can provide valuable insights.

Step 6: Identify Opportunities for Improvement

Identify Strengths and Weaknesses:

- Based on the data and feedback gathered, identify the strengths and weaknesses of your current premium offerings. What aspects are resonating well, and where are there opportunities for improvement?

Evaluate Perks and Tiers:

- Assess the performance of subscription tiers and individual perks. Identify which perks are most valued and if there's a need for adjustments or additions.

Step 7: Implement Changes

Refine Content Strategy:

- Use the insights gained to refine your content strategy. Adjust the frequency and type of premium content based on what resonates most with your audience.

Introduce New Perks:

- Based on subscriber feedback, consider introducing new perks or exclusive benefits that align with subscriber preferences. This could include virtual events, merchandise, or additional content formats.

Adjust Subscription Tiers:

- If necessary, make adjustments to subscription tiers. This might involve adding new tiers with enhanced benefits or modifying existing tiers to better cater to subscriber needs.

Step 8: Communicate Changes

Communicate Transparently:

- Clearly communicate any changes to your premium offerings to your subscribers. Highlight the improvements, new perks, or adjustments to ensure transparency and manage expectations.

Step 9: Repeat the Process

Continuous Improvement:

- Make the evaluation and feedback process an ongoing part of your strategy. The needs and preferences of your audience may evolve, and continuous improvement ensures your premium offerings stay relevant.

By regularly assessing the performance of your premium offerings and gathering feedback from subscribers, you can maintain a dynamic and responsive subscription model that aligns with the evolving preferences of your audience.

11. Communicate Value Effectively: Clearly communicate the value proposition of your premium subscriptions. Highlight the unique content, experiences, and benefits that subscribers receive, emphasizing why it's worth their investment.

Effectively communicating the value proposition of your premium subscriptions is crucial to attract and retain subscribers. Here's a step-by-step guide on how to clearly communicate the unique content, experiences, and benefits that make your premium subscriptions worthwhile:

Step 1: Clearly Define Your Value Proposition

Identify Key Offerings:
- Clearly define what your premium subscription includes. This could be exclusive content, early access, personalized experiences, merchandise, or any other perks.

Highlight Unique Selling Points (USPs):

- Identify the unique aspects that set your premium subscriptions apart from free content or other offerings. What makes it special? Emphasize these USPs in your communication.

Step 2: Craft Compelling Messaging

Create a Clear Tagline:
- Develop a concise and memorable tagline that encapsulates the essence of your premium subscriptions. Make it easy for potential subscribers to understand the value in a single sentence.

Use Clear Language:
- Avoid jargon or industry-specific terms that might confuse potential subscribers. Use language that is straightforward and easy to understand.

Step 3: Develop Engaging Content

Create Engaging Promotional Content:
- Develop promotional content, such as videos, graphics, or written materials, that vividly communicates the benefits of your premium subscriptions. Showcase snippets of exclusive content or behind-the-scenes footage.

Tell Compelling Stories:
- Use storytelling to illustrate the impact of premium content or experiences on subscribers' lives. Share success stories, testimonials, or anecdotes that resonate with your target audience.

Step 4: Clearly Outline Benefits

List Clear Benefits:
- Create a straightforward list of benefits that premium subscribers will enjoy. This could include ad-free content, early access, exclusive interviews, community access, merchandise, and more.

Quantify Value:
- Quantify the value of your premium subscriptions. For example, calculate the monetary value of exclusive content or the savings subscribers get compared to purchasing individual items.

Step 5: Create a Dedicated Landing Page

Design a Dedicated Landing Page:
- Develop a dedicated landing page on your website specifically for premium subscriptions. This page should provide a comprehensive overview of the offerings, benefits, and how to subscribe.

Use Visuals and Graphics:
- Incorporate visuals and graphics that highlight the premium content and perks. Visual elements can make the value proposition more engaging and memorable.

Step 6: Utilize Social Proof

Share Testimonials:
- Feature testimonials from current premium subscribers. Allow them to share their positive experiences and how the premium content has

added value to their lives.

Showcase Subscriber Numbers:

- If you have a significant number of premium subscribers, showcase this as social proof. Large subscriber numbers can indicate the trust and satisfaction of your audience.

Step 7: Leverage Influencers or Partnerships

Partner with Influencers:

- Collaborate with influencers or industry experts who can vouch for the value of your premium subscriptions. Their endorsement can add credibility and reach a broader audience.

Highlight Collaborations:

- If you have collaborations or partnerships that bring additional value to premium subscribers, showcase these in your communication.

Step 8: Provide Clear Subscription Tiers

Tiered Subscription Structure:

- If applicable, create tiered subscription structures with varying levels of benefits. Clearly outline what each tier offers to help subscribers choose the level that best fits their preferences and budget.

Offer a Free Trial:

- Consider offering a free trial period for premium subscriptions. This allows potential subscribers to experience the value firsthand before making a commitment.

Step 9: Regularly Reinforce Value

Regularly Communicate Updates:
- Keep subscribers informed about new content, perks, or experiences regularly. Reinforce the ongoing value they receive as premium subscribers.

Highlight Exclusivity:
- Emphasize the exclusivity of premium content and experiences. The feeling of exclusivity enhances the perceived value of premium subscriptions.

Step 10: Monitor and Adapt

Gather Feedback:
- Encourage feedback from subscribers about their experience with premium content. Use this feedback to make improvements and refine your value proposition.

Monitor Industry Trends:
- Stay informed about industry trends and adjust your value proposition as needed. Adapting to evolving preferences ensures your premium subscriptions remain attractive to your audience.

By following these steps, you can effectively communicate the value proposition of your premium subscriptions, making it clear to potential subscribers why investing in your premium offerings is a worthwhile decision.

12. <u>Maintain Consistency:</u> Consistency is key to retaining premium subscribers. Deliver exclusive content and perks regularly, adhering to the promised schedule. This consistency builds trust and reinforces the value of their ongoing subscription.

Consistency is indeed crucial for retaining premium subscribers. Here's a guide on how to maintain a consistent and reliable delivery of exclusive content and perks:

Step 1: Establish a Clear Schedule

Define Content Release Schedule:
- Clearly define when premium content will be released. This could be a specific day of the week, bi-weekly, or monthly. Communicate this schedule to your subscribers.

Step 2: Plan Content in Advance

Content Calendar:
- Create a content calendar that outlines upcoming premium content releases and events. Planning in advance allows you to maintain consistency without last-minute rushes.

Batch Content Creation:
- Consider batching content creation sessions. Create multiple pieces of content in one go, helping you stay ahead of your schedule and ensuring a consistent flow of material.

Step 3: Leverage Automation

Use Automation Tools:
- Utilize automation tools to schedule content releases. This helps in maintaining consistency even if you're not physically available to publish content at the specified times.

Step 4: Communicate Clearly

Set Subscriber Expectations:
- Clearly communicate the content release schedule to your subscribers when they join. Let them know what to expect and when to anticipate new exclusive content or perks.

Regularly Update Subscribers:
- If there are changes to the schedule or delays, communicate these changes promptly. Transparency helps in maintaining trust even if there are occasional deviations.

Step 5: Diversify Content Types

Offer Varied Content Types:
- Keep the content fresh and engaging by offering a variety of content types. This could include interviews, behind-the-scenes footage, bonus episodes, or exclusive Q&A sessions.

Step 6: Engage with Your Community

Encourage Community Engagement:
- Foster a sense of community among your premium subscribers. Encourage them to provide feedback, suggestions, and engage with each other. A thriving community can be a motivator for consistent content delivery.

Step 7: Incorporate Feedback

Listen to Subscriber Feedback:
- Pay attention to feedback from your premium subscribers. Use their input to refine your

content strategy and ensure that you are delivering the type of content they find valuable.

Step 8: Regularly Assess Performance

Evaluate Content Performance:
- Regularly assess the performance of your exclusive content. Analyze metrics such as engagement, download numbers, and subscriber feedback to understand what resonates with your audience.

Adjust Based on Performance:
- If certain types of content are particularly well-received, consider producing more of that content. Conversely, if certain aspects are not meeting expectations, adapt and make improvements.

Step 9: Introduce Surprises

Occasional Surprises:
- While adhering to a schedule is crucial, occasionally introducing surprises or bonuses can add an extra layer of excitement for your premium subscribers.

Step 10: Stay Adaptive

Adapt to Evolving Trends:
- Stay aware of trends in your niche or industry. Be willing to adapt your content strategy to meet evolving subscriber preferences and expectations.

Step 11: Regularly Communicate Value

Remind Subscribers of Benefits:
- Regularly remind your premium subscribers of the value they receive. This could include exclusive access, early releases, or other perks that set their subscription apart.

Showcase Subscriber Benefits:
- Use your communication channels (podcast episodes, newsletters, social media) to showcase the benefits of being a premium subscriber. Reinforce the value proposition regularly.

Consistency not only involves delivering content on time but also maintaining a high level of quality and engagement. By following these steps, you can build and sustain trust among your premium subscribers, enhancing their overall subscription experience.

By implementing these strategies, you can successfully offer premium or exclusive content to subscribers who pay a monthly fee, creating a sustainable revenue stream while deepening the connection with your most loyal audience members.

CHAPTER 7

Crowdfunding

Crowdfunding is a method of raising capital or funding for a project, venture, or cause by collecting small amounts of money from a large number of people, typically via the internet. It is a way for individuals, businesses, or organizations to fund their ideas, products, or initiatives without relying solely on traditional sources such as banks or investors.

The process involves creating a crowdfunding campaign on a dedicated platform or website, where the project creator sets a funding goal and a deadline. People who are interested in supporting the project can contribute money in exchange for rewards or incentives, which are usually tiered based on the amount of money contributed. These incentives can range from early access to the product or service, exclusive merchandise, or other perks.

There are several types of crowdfunding models, including:

1. **<u>Reward-Based Crowdfunding:</u>** Contributors receive rewards or products in return for their financial support. This is the most common form of crowdfunding.

Reward-based crowdfunding is a dynamic fundraising approach that empowers individuals, businesses, or creative projects to secure financial support from a broad audience. In this model, project creators set a funding goal and a specified timeframe for their campaign on dedicated platforms like Kickstarter or Indiegogo. Backers who resonate with the project's vision and goals contribute funds, and in return, they receive tiered rewards or incentives based on their level of financial support. These rewards can range from early access to the product or service being developed, exclusive merchandise, or personalized experiences. This mutually beneficial exchange not only provides the necessary capital for the project but also fosters a sense of community and collaboration between creators and their supporters. Reward-based crowdfunding has proven to be an effective way to test market interest, validate ideas, and build a loyal customer base, all while offering backers a tangible connection to the projects they believe in.

Reward-based crowdfunding involves several key steps to create and launch a successful campaign. Here's a guide on how to engage in reward-based crowdfunding:

Define Your Project:
- Clearly articulate your project, product, or idea. Describe its purpose, uniqueness, and the potential impact it could have.

Set a Funding Goal:
- Determine the amount of money you need to bring your project to life. Be realistic and consider all the costs associated with production, marketing, and fulfillment of rewards.

Choose the Right Platform:
- Select a crowdfunding platform that aligns with your project's nature and goals. Popular platforms for reward-based crowdfunding include Kickstarter, Indiegogo, and GoFundMe.

Create a Compelling Campaign Page:

- Craft a compelling and visually appealing campaign page. Use high-quality images, videos, and engaging content to effectively communicate your project's story, objectives, and the rewards you're offering.

Set Reward Tiers:

- Design a range of attractive reward tiers that correspond to different contribution levels. Make sure the rewards are appealing and provide value to backers. Consider limited edition or early bird offers to encourage early support.

Establish a Realistic Timeline:

- Set a reasonable campaign duration. Most campaigns run for 30 days, but the optimal duration can vary based on your project's nature. A sense of urgency can drive backers to act, but ensure it's long enough to reach a broader audience.

Promote Your Campaign:

- Leverage social media, email newsletters, and any other relevant channels to spread the word about your campaign. Engage with your community, friends, and family to create initial momentum.

Provide Regular Updates:

- Keep your backers informed with regular updates about the progress of your campaign. Share behind-the-scenes content, milestones achieved, and any adjustments to your plans.

Interact with Backers:

- Respond promptly to comments, messages, and inquiries from your backers. Building a sense of community and keeping an open line of communication can enhance trust and support.

Fulfill Rewards on Time:
- Once the campaign concludes, fulfill your promises by delivering rewards to backers in a timely manner. Transparency and reliability are crucial for maintaining trust within the crowdfunding community.

Express Gratitude:
- Acknowledge and thank your backers for their support. Showing gratitude fosters a positive relationship and may encourage them to support your future endeavors.

By following these steps, you can navigate the reward-based crowdfunding process and increase the likelihood of a successful campaign for your project.

2. <u>Equity Crowdfunding:</u> Investors receive equity (ownership) in the company in exchange for their investment. This is more common for startups and small businesses.

Equity crowdfunding is a financial model that enables businesses, typically startups and small enterprises, to raise capital by selling ownership stakes to a large number of investors through online platforms. In this form of crowdfunding, investors receive shares or equity in the company in exchange for their financial contributions. Unlike traditional crowdfunding, where backers receive rewards or products, equity crowdfunding allows individuals to become shareholders and potentially participate in the company's success. This model democratizes investment by providing opportunities for a diverse range of investors to support and potentially profit from early-stage businesses. Equity crowdfunding platforms, such as Crowdcube and Seedrs, facilitate these transactions, providing a space for businesses to pitch their ideas and for investors to discover and invest in promising ventures. While it offers new funding avenues for startups, equity crowdfunding also involves regulatory considerations to protect both investors and businesses, varying by jurisdiction.

Participating in equity crowdfunding involves several key steps. Here's a guide on how to engage in equity crowdfunding:

Prepare Your Business:
- Ensure that your business is well-prepared for equity crowdfunding. Have a solid business plan, financial projections, and a clear value proposition. Be ready to communicate effectively about your company's potential and growth prospects.

Choose the Right Equity Crowdfunding Platform:
- Select a reputable equity crowdfunding platform that aligns with your business and target audience. Different platforms may cater to specific industries or types of businesses.

Determine Your Funding Goal:
- Establish the amount of capital you need and set a realistic funding goal. Clearly outline how the funds will be used to achieve your business objectives.

Define Your Valuation:
- Determine the valuation of your company. This is the price at which you are willing to sell equity. It's crucial to strike a balance between attracting investors and offering a fair deal for your company's value.

Create a Compelling Campaign:
- Develop a compelling campaign page on the crowdfunding platform. Use professional visuals, articulate your business story, and clearly outline the investment terms and potential

returns for investors.

Engage Potential Investors:

- Leverage your existing network and actively market your campaign. Engage with potential investors through social media, newsletters, and other communication channels. Consider hosting webinars or virtual events to showcase your business and answer questions.

Comply with Regulations:

- Understand and comply with the regulations governing equity crowdfunding in your jurisdiction. This may involve working with legal professionals to ensure that your campaign adheres to all applicable laws.

Offer Incentives:

- While investors are primarily motivated by the potential for financial returns, consider offering additional incentives, such as exclusive perks or discounts, to attract and retain investors.

Provide Regular Updates:

- Keep your investors informed with regular updates on the progress of your business. Transparency is crucial for maintaining trust, and it demonstrates your commitment to achieving the goals outlined in your campaign.

Fulfill Legal and Financial Obligations:

- Once your campaign is successful, fulfill any legal and financial obligations to your investors. This may include issuing share certificates, providing regular financial reports, and adhering to any other commitments made during the campaign.

Build and Maintain Relationships:

- Cultivate a relationship with your investors beyond the campaign. Regularly update them on your business's milestones and achievements, fostering a sense of community and loyalty.

By following these steps, you can navigate the equity crowdfunding process, attract investors, and secure the capital needed to propel your business forward. Keep in mind that equity crowdfunding involves legal and financial complexities, so seeking professional advice is often advisable.

3. <u>Debt Crowdfunding (Crowdlending)</u>: Contributors provide funds as a loan to the project or business, and they receive repayments with interest over time.

Debt crowdfunding, often known as crowdlending, is a financial model where individuals or businesses secure funds by borrowing from a large pool of people through online crowdfunding platforms. In this arrangement, borrowers create campaigns specifying the amount they need, the purpose of the loan, and the proposed interest rate and repayment terms. Investors then choose projects to fund, contributing various amounts to collectively meet the borrower's financial target. Unlike equity crowdfunding, where investors receive ownership stakes, in debt crowdfunding, investors receive returns in the form of regular interest payments as the borrower repays the loan over a predefined period. This model provides an alternative financing avenue for borrowers without diluting ownership, while investors gain the potential for steady returns. Crowdlending platforms facilitate the entire process, serving as intermediaries and fostering a direct connection between borrowers and lenders.

Engaging in debt crowdfunding, or crowdlending, involves several key steps. Here's a guide on how to navigate the process:

Define Your Funding Needs: Clearly articulate the purpose of the loan, the amount needed, and the specific terms of repayment. Provide detailed information about your project, business, or personal circumstances.

Defining your funding needs is a critical aspect of any fundraising or crowdfunding effort. To effectively communicate your financial requirements, start by identifying the specific purpose for which you seek funding, whether it be launching a new product, expanding a business, covering medical expenses, or realizing a creative project. Conduct a thorough cost analysis, breaking down all associated expenses, and set a realistic funding goal that encompasses production, marketing, operational costs, and any platform fees. Consider potential contingencies and communicate milestones or distinct phases if applicable. Transparency is key, so explain how you arrived at your funding goal, offering a detailed breakdown of costs and demonstrating responsible financial planning. Use engaging visuals, such as charts or videos, to enhance your presentation, and offer different contribution levels with corresponding benefits to provide backers with options. Craft a compelling story around your funding needs, sharing the journey and impact of your project to emotionally engage potential backers. Through these steps, you can create a transparent, persuasive narrative that resonates with your audience and increases the likelihood of a successful fundraising campaign.

Select a Crowdlending Platform: Choose a reputable crowdlending platform that aligns with your funding needs. Different platforms cater to various types of borrowers, so select one that best suits your situation.

Create a Compelling Campaign:
- Develop a persuasive campaign on the chosen platform. Clearly explain why you need the loan, how you plan to use the funds, and the potential benefits for lenders. Be transparent about your financial situation and present a well-thought-out plan for loan repayment.

Set Loan Terms:
- Determine the interest rate, loan duration, and any other relevant terms. Ensure that the terms are competitive and fair, taking into account both the borrower's needs and the expectations of potential lenders.

Market Your Campaign:
- Actively promote your campaign through various channels, such as social media, email newsletters, and any other networks you have. Engage with potential lenders, answer questions, and provide updates to build trust and credibility.

Communicate Effectively:
- Clearly communicate the potential risks and rewards of investing in your loan. Provide regular updates on the progress of your campaign and any developments related to your project or circumstances.

Comply with Regulations:
- Be aware of and comply with any regulations governing crowdlending in your jurisdiction. Different regions may have specific legal requirements to protect both borrowers and lenders.

Respond to Investor Inquiries:
- Promptly respond to inquiries and messages

from potential lenders. Building trust and maintaining open communication is crucial in securing support for your campaign.

Fulfill Loan Repayment Obligations:
- Once your campaign is successful, adhere to the agreed-upon repayment schedule. Ensure timely payments to fulfill your financial obligations to the lenders.

Express Gratitude:
- Show appreciation to your lenders. Consider expressing your gratitude through personalized messages, updates, or even offering exclusive perks to those who supported your campaign.

By following these steps, you can effectively navigate the debt crowdfunding process and increase your chances of a successful crowdlending campaign. Remember to approach the process with transparency, honesty, and a well-thought-out plan for using the funds and repaying the loan. Additionally, seeking professional advice and understanding the legal and financial implications is advisable.

4. <u>Donation-Based Crowdfunding:</u> Contributors make donations without expecting financial returns or rewards. This is often used for charitable or personal causes.

Popular crowdfunding platforms include Kickstarter, Indiegogo, GoFundMe, and Crowdcube, among others. Crowdfunding has become a popular way for individuals and businesses to access capital, test market interest, and engage with their community of supporters.

Here's an example of how to structure a donation-based crowdfunding campaign for your podcast:

🎙 [*Your Podcast Name*] Crowdfunding Campaign: Amplifying the Sound of Stories

Dear [*Podcast Community Name*],

We're reaching out to you, our amazing listeners and supporters, with an exciting opportunity to be an integral part of the future of [Your Podcast Name]. Over the years, your enthusiasm and encouragement have fueled our passion for storytelling, and now we invite you to join us in taking our podcast to new heights through a donation-based crowdfunding campaign.

Why Crowdfunding Matters:

[Your Podcast Name] has been a labor of love, and we've been fortunate to have you by our side on this journey. However, to continue creating the content you love and exploring new avenues, we need your support. Crowdfunding allows us to:

- Enhance Production Quality: *Upgrade our recording equipment, ensuring crystal-clear sound and a more immersive listening experience.*

- Expand Content Variety: *Bring more diverse stories, interviews, and expert insights to your ears by broadening our content scope.*

- Connect Deeper: *Build a stronger community by organizing live events, Q&A sessions, and engaging with you on a more personal level.*

How You Can Support [Your Podcast Name]:

1. Visit Our Crowdfunding Page:

- *[Link to Crowdfunding Page]*

2. Choose Your Support Level:

- *Select a donation tier that resonates with you. Every contribution, no matter the size, plays a crucial role.*

Exclusive Supporter Perks:

- Bronze Contributor ($10):

- *Your name featured on our website's Wall of Gratitude and a personalized thank-you email.*

- Silver Advocate ($25):

- *Early access to select episodes, a shout-out on the podcast, and all previous rewards.*

- Gold Pioneer ($50):

- *Exclusive access to a monthly live Q&A session with our hosts, a limited edition podcast sticker, and all previous rewards.*

Our Milestone Goals:

- $2,000: Launch of a Special Series

- $5,000: Podcast Studio Upgrade for Enhanced Sound Quality

Stay Connected During the Campaign:

- Social Media:

- *Follow us on [Social Media Platforms] for campaign updates, behind-the-scenes glimpses, and interactive polls.*

- Podcast Episodes:

- *We'll be sharing campaign updates in our episodes, keeping you informed about the progress.*

Join Us in Amplifying the Sound of Stories!

Your support has been the heartbeat of [Your Podcast Name], and together, we can amplify the sound of stories and create a podcasting experience that resonates even more deeply with you, our cherished community.

Thank you for being the most crucial part of our podcast family.

With gratitude,

[Your Podcast Team]

[Link to Crowdfunding Page]

This example provides a structured approach to a donation-based crowdfunding campaign for a podcast, emphasizing the reasons for crowdfunding, different support levels, exclusive perks, milestone goals, and ways for supporters to stay connected during the campaign.

CHAPTER 8

Organize live podcast events

Organizing live events for your podcast can be an exciting way to connect with your audience in real-time and generate revenue through admission fees. Here's a step-by-step guide on how to organize live podcast events:

Step 1: Define the Purpose and Format

Identify the Purpose:
- Determine the goal of your live event. Is it a Q&A session, a special interview, a live recording, or a webinar on a specific topic?

Choose the Format:
- Decide on the format that aligns with your content and engages your audience effectively. This could include live interviews, interactive discussions, audience Q&A, or a combination.

Step 2: Select a Platform

Choose a Hosting Platform:
- Select a platform for hosting your live event. Options include Zoom, Crowdcast, YouTube Live, or dedicated webinar platforms. Ensure the platform supports your desired format and audience size.

Set Up Registration:
- If applicable, set up a registration process to

capture attendee information and manage admission. Some platforms offer built-in registration features.

Step 3: Plan and Promote

Create a Detailed Plan:
- Outline the event schedule, including key segments, breaks, and interactive elements. Plan how you'll engage with the audience and keep the content engaging.

Promote the Event:
- Start promoting the live event well in advance. Utilize your podcast episodes, social media, email newsletters, and website to create anticipation. Clearly communicate the value attendees will receive.

Step 4: Ticketing and Admission

Set Admission Fees:
- Determine the admission fee based on the value of the event and your audience's willingness to pay. Consider offering early bird discounts or bundled packages.

Choose a Ticketing Platform:
- Use a reliable ticketing platform like Eventbrite, Ticket Tailor, or a built-in option from your hosting platform. Ensure it integrates seamlessly with your chosen event platform.

Step 5: Technical Setup

Test Equipment:
- Test your audio and video equipment to ensure

clear, high-quality production. Consider investing in a good microphone and camera for professional results.

Rehearse:

- Conduct a rehearsal to familiarize yourself with the live event setup. Check for any technical glitches and ensure smooth transitions between segments.

Step 6: Engage During the Live Event

Interact with Attendees:

- Encourage audience participation through Q&A sessions, polls, and interactive segments. Make attendees feel involved and valued.

Promote Future Episodes and Events:

- Use the live event as an opportunity to promote upcoming podcast episodes, events, or exclusive content to keep the excitement going.

Step 7: Post-Event Activities

Collect Feedback:

- Gather feedback from attendees to improve future events. Consider sending a post-event survey to understand what worked well and areas for improvement.

Repurpose Content:

- Repurpose highlights from the live event into teaser clips, social media content, or even bonus podcast episodes for those who couldn't attend.

<u>Step 8: Evaluate and Iterate</u>

Analyze Metrics:
- Review attendance numbers, revenue generated, and audience engagement metrics. Use these insights to refine your approach for future live events.

Iterate and Improve:
- Incorporate lessons learned into your future live events. Continuously refine your approach to offer an even better experience for your audience.

By following these steps, you can successfully organize and monetize live podcast events, creating a unique and valuable experience for your audience.

Let's create an example for organizing a live podcast event with an admission fee:

● Podcast Unplugged: A Night of Live Insights

Join us for a one-of-a-kind experience as we bring the magic of [Your Podcast Name] to life in an exclusive live event! "Podcast Unplugged" is not just a show; it's an immersive journey into the stories, conversations, and behind-the-scenes moments that make our podcast special.

Event Details:

- Date & Time:
    - [Date], [Time] (Timezone)
- Venue:

- [Virtual Platform Link]

What to Expect:

- Live Interviews:
    - Get up close and personal with special guests as we dive into topics that go beyond our regular episodes.
- Interactive Q&A:
    - Engage with us in real-time by submitting your questions and comments. We'll respond live during the event.
- Behind-the-Scenes Insights:
    - Discover the making of [Your Podcast Name]. From funny anecdotes to challenges faced, we'll share the untold stories.

Ticket Information:

- Admission Fee:
    - $15 per ticket
- How to Get Tickets:
    - Visit [Ticketing Platform Link] to secure your spot. Limited tickets available, so grab yours now!

Exclusive Perks for Attendees:

- Early Bird Access:
    - First 50 attendees get early access to the virtual venue 15 minutes before the event begins.
- Virtual Meet-and-Greet:
    - A select number of attendees will have the opportunity for a virtual meet-and-greet with

the hosts after the event.

How to Attend:

Purchase Your Ticket:
- Visit [Ticketing Platform Link] and choose your ticket option. Complete the purchase to secure your spot.

Receive Confirmation:
- You'll receive a confirmation email with the virtual event link and details on how to join.

Stay Connected:

- Social Media Hashtag:
  - Use #PodcastUnplugged to share your excitement and connect with other attendees before, during, and after the event.
- Event Updates:
  - Follow us on [Social Media Platforms] for event updates, sneak peeks, and behind-the-scenes teasers.

Join Us for a Night to Remember!

"Podcast Unplugged" is not just an event; it's a celebration of our podcast community. Your support has made [Your Podcast Name] what it is today, and we can't wait to share this unforgettable experience with you.

Thank you for being the heartbeat of our podcast family!

[Your Podcast Team]

[Ticketing Platform Link]

This example provides details for a virtual live podcast event, including the event's purpose, schedule, ticket information, exclusive perks for attendees, and ways to stay connected. It emphasizes the uniqueness of the experience and encourages audience engagement in real-time.

[Ticketing Platform Link]

CHAPTER 9

Selling Courses or Workshops

Creating and selling online courses or workshops related to your podcast content is a great way to monetize your expertise and provide additional value to your audience. Here's a step-by-step guide on how to go about it:

Step 1: Identify Your Expertise

Assess Your Podcast Content:
- Identify specific topics or themes within your podcast where you have expertise and knowledge to share.

Understand Audience Needs:
- Consider what topics or skills your audience is interested in and where they might benefit from deeper insights or practical guidance.

Step 2: Plan Your Course

Define Learning Objectives:
- Clearly outline what participants will learn from your course. Break down the key takeaways and skills they'll acquire.

Course Structure:
- Plan the structure of your course, including modules, lessons, and any supporting materials. Create a logical flow that builds upon each section.

Step 3: Choose a Platform

Select an Online Course Platform:
- Choose a platform that supports the delivery of online courses. Popular options include Teachable, Udemy, Thinkific, or platforms integrated with your podcast website.

Consider Hosting Webinars:
- For a more interactive experience, consider hosting live webinars as part of your course using platforms like Zoom or Crowdcast.

Step 4: Create Engaging Content

Develop Course Content:
- Create engaging content for each module. This could include video lessons, downloadable resources, quizzes, and assignments.

Utilize Podcast Content:
- Repurpose relevant podcast episodes, interviews, or discussions to complement your course content. This provides added value and ties back to your podcast.

Step 5: Set Pricing and Sales Strategy

Pricing Strategy:
- Determine the pricing for your course. Consider your target audience, the value you're providing, and competitive pricing in your niche.

Sales Pages and Marketing:
- Create compelling sales pages that highlight the benefits of your course. Use your podcast, website, and social media to market the course.

Step 6: Offer Bonuses and Incentives

Add Value with Bonuses:
- Provide additional incentives for early sign-ups, such as exclusive access to a live Q&A session, downloadable resources, or a bonus podcast episode.

Step 7: Engage with Participants

Interactive Elements:
- Incorporate interactive elements like discussion forums, live Q&A sessions, or feedback sessions to enhance the learning experience.

Community Building:
- Encourage participants to connect with each other. Consider creating a community space, such as a private Facebook group, for ongoing discussions.

Step 8: Launch and Iterate

Launch Your Course:
- Announce your course through your podcast, email newsletters, and social media channels. Use launch strategies to generate initial interest.

Gather Feedback:
- Collect feedback from participants to understand what worked well and areas for improvement. Use this information to enhance future iterations of your course.

Step 9: Scale and Expand

Scale Your Offerings:

- As you gain experience and feedback, consider expanding your course offerings or creating advanced courses to cater to different skill levels.

Collaborate with Experts:

- Collaborate with other experts or podcast guests to offer joint courses, providing a diverse range of perspectives and expertise.

By following these steps, you can successfully create and sell online courses or workshops related to your podcast content, leveraging your expertise and building a valuable revenue stream.

EXAMPLE: *Let's consider a hypothetical scenario where you run a podcast focused on personal development, specifically addressing topics such as time management, goal setting, and productivity. Your audience has shown a keen interest in these subjects, making it an ideal niche to explore for creating online courses. Here's how you could apply the steps outlined:*

Step 1: Identify Your Expertise

- Podcast Content Assessment: *Review your podcast episodes to identify key areas where you consistently provide valuable insights and practical tips, such as effective time management techniques and goal-setting strategies.*
- Understand Audience Needs: *Analyze listener feedback, reviews, and engagement on social media to determine the specific aspects of time management and productivity that resonate most with your audience.*

Step 2: Plan Your Course

- Define Learning Objectives: *Outline the key skills and*

knowledge participants will gain, such as mastering time-blocking, setting SMART goals, and implementing productivity tools.
- Course Structure: *Plan a course structure that logically progresses from fundamental concepts to more advanced techniques. Consider incorporating real-life examples and case studies to enhance learning.*

Step 3: Choose a Platform

- Select an Online Course Platform: *Opt for a platform like Teachable, where you can easily upload video lessons, organize course materials, and manage participant progress. Ensure seamless integration with your podcast website for a cohesive user experience.*
- Consider Hosting Webinars: *Given the interactive nature of your content, explore hosting live webinars using Zoom to provide additional opportunities for Q&A sessions and engagement.*

Step 4: Create Engaging Content

- Develop Course Content: *Create high-quality video lessons, downloadable templates, and interactive quizzes to cater to different learning styles. Incorporate your podcast insights into each module for a cohesive learning experience.*
- Utilize Podcast Content: *Repurpose relevant podcast episodes or conduct exclusive podcast interviews with experts in time management to supplement your course content.*

Step 5: Set Pricing and Sales Strategy

- Pricing Strategy: *Determine a competitive yet value-driven pricing strategy. Consider offering a limited-time launch discount to incentivize early enrollment.*
- Sales Pages and Marketing: *Craft persuasive sales pages on*

your website and leverage your podcast episodes to market the course. Utilize social media platforms to create anticipation and drive enrollment.

Step 6: Offer Bonuses and Incentives

- Add Value with Bonuses: *Offer bonuses such as access to a private online community, downloadable productivity resources, or a live Q&A session with you as a podcast host.*

Step 7: Engage with Participants

- Interactive Elements: *Implement discussion forums within the course platform, conduct live Q&A sessions, and encourage peer-to-peer interaction to enhance the learning experience.*
- Community Building: *Create a private Facebook group for course participants to foster a sense of community, enabling ongoing discussions and mutual support.*

Step 8: Launch and Iterate

- Launch Your Course: *Announce the course through a dedicated podcast episode, email newsletters, and social media channels. Leverage a launch sequence to build excitement.*
- Gather Feedback: *Actively seek feedback from participants through surveys or discussion forums to identify areas for improvement and refinement.*

Step 9: Scale and Expand

- Scale Your Offerings: *Based on feedback and demand, consider expanding your course offerings to include advanced topics or specialized workshops.*
- Collaborate with Experts: *Explore collaborations with guest*

experts or professionals in related fields to offer joint courses, providing a diverse range of perspectives.

By implementing these steps, you can successfully create and sell online courses aligned with your podcast content, offering valuable insights to your audience while generating a sustainable revenue stream.

CHAPTER 10

Join podcast networks

Joining podcast networks can be a strategic move to connect with advertisers, gain exposure, and explore monetization opportunities. Here's a guide on how to join podcast networks:

1. **Identify Suitable Podcast Networks:**

Research Networks:

- Start by researching podcast networks that align with your podcast's niche, content, and target audience. Look for networks that have a good reputation and a track record of successful partnerships with podcasters.

Consider Your Goals:

- Define your goals for joining a network. Whether it's to increase advertising opportunities, gain access to better production resources, or grow your audience, make sure the network aligns with your objectives.

2. **Prepare Your Podcast:**

Quality Content:

- Ensure your podcast has high-quality content and a consistent release schedule. Networks are more likely to consider podcasts that demonstrate professionalism and dedication to their audience.

Statistics:

- Have clear and updated statistics about your podcast, including listener demographics, download numbers, and any other relevant metrics. Networks often require this information to evaluate potential partners.

3. <u>Reach Out to Networks:</u>

Submit Your Podcast:

- Most podcast networks have a submission process. Visit their websites and follow the instructions to submit your podcast for consideration. Provide relevant information about your podcast, including its niche, target audience, and any notable achievements.

Pitch Your Podcast:

- Craft a compelling pitch that highlights what makes your podcast unique and why it would be a valuable addition to the network. Emphasize your audience size, engagement, and any potential advertising appeal.

4. <u>Negotiate Terms:</u>

Understand Revenue Sharing:

- Some podcast networks offer revenue-sharing arrangements. Understand the terms of these agreements, including the percentage of revenue you'll receive and any other conditions.

Ad Placement:

- Clarify how advertising will be handled. Understand whether you have control over the ads that appear on your podcast or if the network manages this aspect.

5. <u>Assess Network Services:</u>

Additional Services:

- Consider what additional services the network provides. Some networks offer production assistance, promotional support, or access to exclusive events that can benefit your podcast.

Advisory Support:

- Look for networks that provide advisory support or guidance on growing your podcast. Networks with experienced professionals can offer valuable insights and advice.

6. <u>Evaluate Network Reputation:</u>

Reviews and Testimonials:

- Check for reviews or testimonials from other podcasters who have partnered with the network. Assess their experiences, especially regarding the network's reliability, communication, and effectiveness in securing advertising opportunities.

Track Record:

- Look into the network's track record of successfully monetizing podcasts. A network with a history of connecting podcasts with relevant advertisers is more likely to be a fruitful partnership.

7. **Execute Agreements:**

Legal and Contractual Agreements:

- Once you've negotiated terms, carefully review and understand any legal or contractual agreements. Seek legal advice if necessary before committing to any long-term partnership.

8. **Stay Engaged:**

Communication:

- Maintain open communication with the network. Regularly discuss your podcast's performance, potential advertising opportunities, and any concerns or suggestions you may have.

9. **Optimize Monetization:**

Explore Additional Revenue Streams:

- While working with a network, continue exploring additional monetization opportunities, such as sponsorships, affiliate marketing, or listener support.

By following these steps, you can successfully join a podcast network, enhance your monetization opportunities, and potentially connect with advertisers to generate revenue for your podcast.

Let's consider a fictional example of a podcast named "Healthy Habits Haven" hosted by Alex, who is passionate about promoting a healthy lifestyle. Alex decides to join a podcast network to expand the show's reach, connect with advertisers, and explore monetization opportunities.

Podcast: *Healthy Habits Haven*

1. <u>Identify Suitable Podcast Networks:</u>

After researching podcast networks, Alex finds "WellnessWaves Network," a network known for its focus on health and wellness content. The network has a reputation for successfully connecting podcasts with advertisers in the health and fitness industry.

2. <u>Prepare Your Podcast:</u>

Quality Content:

- *Alex ensures the podcast consistently delivers valuable content on topics like nutrition, fitness, mental health, and wellness trends. Episodes are well-researched and cater to a broad audience interested in leading a healthier lifestyle.*

Statistics:

- *Alex gathers statistics, showcasing the podcast's growing listenership, demographics, and positive engagement on social media. Clear insights into the audience help make a compelling case to the network.*

3. <u>Reach Out to Networks:</u>

Submit Your Podcast:

- *Following WellnessWaves Network's submission process, Alex submits "Healthy Habits Haven" for consideration. The submission includes a podcast description, notable episodes, and the show's unique value proposition.*

Pitch Your Podcast:

- *In the pitch, Alex emphasizes the podcast's commitment to promoting a healthy lifestyle, the engaged and diverse audience, and the potential for advertisers in the health and wellness industry to connect with the podcast's community.*

4. <u>Negotiate Terms:</u>

Understand Revenue Sharing:

- *WellnessWaves Network proposes a revenue-sharing model, where Alex will receive 60% of the advertising revenue generated by "Healthy Habits Haven." The terms include a commitment to securing advertisers relevant to the health and wellness niche.*

Ad Placement:

- *Alex retains control over ad placements within the podcast to ensure alignment with the show's content and maintain authenticity.*

5. <u>Assess Network Services:</u>

Additional Services:

- *WellnessWaves Network offers additional services such as promotional support, featuring podcasts in network-wide newsletters, and access to health and wellness events for potential collaboration.*

Advisory Support:

- *Alex is assigned an advertising support advisor who provides insights on optimizing ad-reads, tailoring content to attract advertisers, and navigating potential challenges in the health and wellness advertising space.*

6. <u>Evaluate Network Reputation:</u>

Reviews and Testimonials:

- *Alex reads positive testimonials from other health and wellness podcasters in WellnessWaves Network, praising the network's dedication to promoting well-being and fostering successful partnerships.*

Track Record:

- *The network showcases a track record of successfully connecting podcasts with reputable advertisers in the health and wellness industry, resulting in increased monetization for its podcasters.*

7. <u>Execute Agreements:</u>

Legal and Contractual Agreements:

- *After a thorough review, Alex signs a contractual agreement with WellnessWaves Network, detailing revenue-sharing terms, ad placement guidelines, and the duration of the partnership.*

8. <u>Stay Engaged:</u>

Communication:

- *Alex maintains regular communication with the network, participating in network-wide events, and staying informed about potential advertising opportunities or trends in the health and wellness space.*

9. <u>Optimize Monetization:</u>

Explore Additional Revenue Streams:

- *While benefiting from the network's advertising partnerships, Alex explores additional revenue streams, such as partnerships with health and wellness brands for affiliate marketing and collaborations with fitness influencers.*

In this example, Alex strategically joins WellnessWaves Network, leveraging its expertise in the health and wellness industry to connect with advertisers, gain exposure, and explore various avenues for monetizing "Healthy Habits Haven."

CHAPTER 11

Subscription Model

*I*ntroducing a subscription model for your podcast on platforms like Apple Podcasts and Spotify involves careful planning and execution. Here's a step-by-step guide on how to do it:

Define Your Value Proposition:
- Clearly outline what exclusive benefits subscribers will receive. This could include ad-free episodes, bonus content, early access to episodes, or other perks.

Choose the Right Platforms:
- Leverage platforms like Apple Podcasts and Spotify that offer subscription features. Familiarize yourself with the requirements and guidelines of each platform.

Determine Subscription Tiers:
- Plan different subscription tiers based on the value provided. For instance, a basic tier might offer ad-free episodes, while a premium tier could include exclusive interviews or

behind-the-scenes content.

Set Pricing:

- Research similar podcasts in your niche and determine a competitive pricing structure. Ensure that the price aligns with the value you're offering to subscribers.

Engage with Listeners:

- Communicate the upcoming subscription model to your audience through podcast episodes, social media, and your website. Clearly explain the benefits of subscribing and encourage feedback.

Implement Subscription Model:

- Utilize the subscription features on Apple Podcasts and Spotify to set up the different tiers. Follow the platform-specific guidelines for creating engaging visuals and descriptions.

Launch Campaign:

- Dedicate podcast episodes to announce the launch of your subscription model. Create teaser content, countdowns, and promotional posts on social media to build anticipation.

Provide Exclusive Content:

- Consistently deliver on the promises made to subscribers. Ensure that exclusive content is of high quality and aligns with the interests of your audience.

Monitor Analytics:

- Regularly review subscription analytics provided by the platforms. Track subscriber numbers, engagement rates, and other relevant metrics to assess the success of your subscription model.

Engage with Subscribers:

- Foster a sense of community among your subscribers. Consider creating a private online group, hosting live Q&A sessions, or offering exclusive interactions to show appreciation.

Gather and Adapt Based on Feedback:

- Actively seek feedback from subscribers and adjust your content or subscription model based on their suggestions. This shows your commitment to providing value and improving the subscriber experience.

By following these steps, you can successfully introduce a subscription model for your podcast, offering a premium experience to your subscribers while exploring new revenue streams for your content.

Let's explore a hypothetical example of a podcast named "Travel Tales Unplugged" hosted by Emily, a seasoned traveler sharing unique stories and travel tips. Emily decides to introduce a subscription model to provide her audience with an ad-free experience and exclusive travel guides.

Podcast: Travel Tales Unplugged

1. Define Your Value Proposition:

Ad-Free Experience:

- The subscription model for "Travel Tales Unplugged" offers an ad-free listening experience to subscribers, ensuring an immersive journey through each episode without interruptions.

Exclusive Travel Guides:

- Subscribers gain access to monthly travel guides curated by Emily. These guides include insider tips, off-the-beaten-path recommendations, and exclusive insights not shared in regular episodes.

2. Choose Subscription Platforms:

Leverage Apple Podcasts and Spotify:

- Emily decides to leverage Apple Podcasts and Spotify, both actively exploring subscription models. These platforms provide a wide reach and convenient subscription features.

Seamless Integration:

- Emily ensures a seamless integration of the subscription model with these platforms, utilizing the in-app subscription features provided.

3. Plan Subscription Tiers:

Basic Tier:

- The basic subscription tier, priced at $4.99 per month, grants listeners an ad-free experience for regular episodes of "Travel Tales Unplugged."

Premium Tier:

- The premium subscription tier, priced at $9.99 per month, includes ad-free episodes, access to exclusive travel guides, and early releases of upcoming episodes.

4. <u>Set Pricing</u>:

Research and Positioning:

- Emily conducts research on pricing models for other travel podcasts and evaluates the unique value she provides. The pricing is set to align with the podcast's quality and the additional benefits offered.

Communicate Value:

- In her promotional materials and announcements, Emily clearly communicates the value of the subscription tiers, emphasizing the enhanced listening experience and the insider knowledge provided in the exclusive travel guides.

5. <u>Engage with Listeners</u>:

Podcast Announcements:

- Emily uses dedicated podcast episodes to announce the introduction of the subscription model, explaining the benefits and encouraging her audience to participate.

Social Media Campaign:

- Emily runs a social media campaign leading up to the

launch, posting teaser content, behind-the-scenes glimpses, and engaging with her audience to build excitement.

6. <u>Implement Subscription Model</u>:

Platform Features:

- Emily utilizes the subscription features available on Apple Podcasts and Spotify to set up and launch the subscription model.

Visual Branding:

- Engaging visuals, graphics, and branding materials are created to showcase the subscription tiers and communicate the value proposition to potential subscribers.

7. <u>Launch Campaign</u>:

Dedicated Launch Episode:

- Emily releases a dedicated podcast episode to officially launch the subscription model. In this episode, she explains the benefits, shares the subscription tiers, and encourages her listeners to join the premium tier.

Countdown and Teasers:

- In the weeks leading up to the launch, Emily creates countdowns, teaser content, and promotional posts on social media platforms to generate anticipation and interest.

8. <u>Provide Exclusive Content:</u>

Consistent Delivery:

- Emily consistently delivers on the promises made to subscribers. Premium subscribers enjoy ad-free regular episodes and eagerly anticipate each month's exclusive travel guide.

Engagement Strategies:

- To maintain engagement, Emily actively seeks feedback from subscribers, conducts polls to understand travel preferences, and considers subscriber suggestions for future content.

9. <u>Monitor and Adjust:</u>

Analytics Review:

- Regularly monitoring subscription analytics on Apple Podcasts and Spotify, Emily assesses subscriber numbers, engagement rates, and other relevant metrics.

Adaptation:

- Emily remains adaptable, adjusting her content strategy or subscription model based on subscriber feedback, changing travel trends, and emerging destinations.

10. <u>Engage with Subscribers:</u>

Exclusive Community:

- Emily creates a private online community or forum exclusively for subscribers, fostering a sense of community among travel enthusiasts who value the podcast.

Acknowledgments and Rewards:

- Emily acknowledges and rewards subscribers, perhaps through personalized shout-outs in episodes, special access to live Q&A sessions, or exclusive travel-related giveaways.

In this example, Emily successfully introduces a subscription model for "Travel Tales Unplugged," offering listeners an enhanced experience with ad-free content and exclusive travel guides. Through strategic planning and engagement efforts, Emily aims to build a dedicated subscriber base while exploring new monetization avenues.

CHAPTER 12

License your podcast content for a fee

*L*icensing your podcast content to other platforms or media outlets can be a strategic move to expand your reach and generate additional revenue. *Here's a step-by-step guide on how to license your podcast content:*

Assess Your Content:

- Evaluate your podcast content to identify episodes or series that have high-quality and broad appeal. Consider the evergreen nature of the content, as this can make it more attractive for licensing.

Understand Licensing Terms:

- Familiarize yourself with licensing terms and agreements. Determine whether you want to offer exclusive or non-exclusive licenses, the duration of the license, and the territories covered.

Identify Potential Partners:

- Research potential partners, including other podcast platforms, media outlets, or organizations that align with your content and target audience. Look for entities that have a substantial audience base and can benefit from your content.

Create a Licensing Proposal:

- Develop a comprehensive licensing proposal that outlines the terms, conditions, and benefits of licensing your podcast content. Highlight the unique aspects of your content, its target audience, and how it can enhance the partner's offerings.

Set Pricing and Terms:

- Determine a fair pricing structure for licensing your content. Consider factors such as the size of the partner's audience, the exclusivity of the license, and the potential impact on your own brand.

Reach Out to Potential Partners:

- Initiate contact with potential partners through professional outreach. Craft personalized emails or proposals that clearly communicate the value of your podcast content and how it can benefit their platform or audience.

Negotiate and Finalize Agreements:

- Engage in negotiations with interested parties. Be open to discussions on terms, pricing, and any specific requirements they may have. Once an agreement is reached, formalize the licensing arrangement through a written contract.

Provide Access to Content:

- Deliver the agreed-upon podcast content to the partner in the specified format. Ensure that the transfer is seamless, and provide any necessary support or materials to assist in the integration of your content onto their platform.

Promote the Partnership:

- Collaborate with the partner to promote the licensing partnership. Utilize your social media, newsletters, and podcast episodes to inform your audience about the expanded availability of your content on the partner's platform.

Monitor Performance:

- Regularly monitor the performance of your content on the partner's platform. Track metrics such as downloads, listener engagement, and audience growth to assess the impact of the licensing agreement.

Renew or Explore New Opportunities:

- If the licensing arrangement proves successful, consider renewing the agreement or exploring similar opportunities with other partners. Use the experience to refine your licensing strategy and maximize the potential of your podcast content.

Remember to consult with legal professionals when drafting licensing agreements to ensure that your rights and interests are protected. Licensing your podcast content can be a mutually beneficial arrangement, providing additional exposure and revenue while expanding your audience reach.

Let's create an example with a podcast named "Adventure Explorers" hosted by Chris Anderson, an experienced traveler and adventurer. Chris decides to license his podcast content to a travel media platform, "Global Journeys," for syndication. Here's a step-by-step example:

Podcast: *Adventure Explorers*

1. Assess Your Content:

- Chris reviews the "Adventure Explorers" podcast episodes and identifies a series focusing on unique and off-the-beaten-path travel destinations that has consistently captivated his audience.

2. Understand Licensing Terms:

- Chris opts to offer an exclusive license to "Global Journeys" for a duration of one year. This exclusive arrangement ensures that the travel media platform receives unique content, and Chris retains the ability to explore other licensing opportunities in the future.

3. Identify Potential Partner:

- "Global Journeys" is selected as the ideal partner due to its broad audience interested in immersive travel experiences. The platform expresses a keen interest in enriching its travel podcast category with Chris's firsthand adventures.

4. <u>Create a Licensing Proposal:</u>

- Chris prepares a comprehensive licensing proposal outlining the terms of the agreement. The proposal highlights the engaging storytelling in each episode, the broad appeal of the destinations covered, and the potential for increased engagement on "Global Journeys."

5. <u>Set Pricing and Terms:</u>

- A fair pricing structure is determined based on the number of episodes licensed and the potential impact on "Global Journeys' " audience growth. Terms include exclusivity, promotional considerations, and regular reporting on performance metrics.

6. <u>Reach Out to "Global Journeys":</u>

- Chris reaches out to the content acquisition team at "Global Journeys" through a well-crafted email, attaching the licensing proposal. The email emphasizes the unique aspects of "Adventure Explorers" and its potential to enhance the travel platform's podcast offerings.

7. <u>Negotiate and Finalize Agreements:</u>

- Following positive discussions, Chris engages in negotiations with the content acquisition team at "Global Journeys." They discuss specific terms, pricing adjustments, and any additional requirements. Once both parties reach an agreement, a formal licensing contract is drafted and signed.

8. <u>Provide Access to Content:</u>

- Chris collaborates with his podcast hosting platform to securely provide access to the agreed-upon episodes in the required format. He ensures a smooth transfer and offers support to facilitate the integration of the content onto "Global Journeys' " platform.

9. <u>Promote the Partnership:</u>

- Both "Adventure Explorers" and "Global Journeys" collaborate on promotional efforts. Chris announces the syndication partnership in podcast episodes, on his website, and through social media channels. "Global Journeys" promotes the addition of "Adventure Explorers" to its travel podcast lineup across its media outlets.

10. <u>Monitor Performance:</u>

- Chris and "Global Journeys" regularly monitor the performance of the syndicated content. They track download numbers, listener engagement, and audience feedback to evaluate the success of the partnership.

11. <u>Renew or Explore New Opportunities:</u>

- If the syndication proves successful for both parties, Chris and "Global Journeys" may discuss the possibility of renewing the licensing agreement. Simultaneously, Chris explores similar opportunities with other travel platforms to further expand the reach of "Adventure Explorers."

In this example, Chris Anderson successfully licenses a series of "Adventure Explorers" episodes to "Global Journeys," creating a collaborative partnership that elevates the reach of his travel content and provides an additional revenue stream through licensing fees.

CHAPTER 13

Consulting Services

Offering consulting or coaching services based on your podcast expertise can be a rewarding way to monetize your knowledge and provide personalized assistance to your audience. Here's a step-by-step guide on how to go about it:

Identify Your Expertise:
- Assess the content of your podcast and identify specific areas where you have expertise. This could be in-depth knowledge on a particular industry, skill set, or niche that aligns with your podcast theme.

Understand Audience Needs:
- Analyze your audience's feedback, questions, and engagement to understand their needs. Identify common challenges or areas where they seek guidance and support related to the topics you cover in your podcast.

Define Your Consulting/Coaching Offerings:
- Clearly define the consulting or coaching services you will offer. This could include one-on-one sessions, group coaching, workshops, or specialized consulting packages. Outline the specific deliverables and benefits

clients can expect.

Set Pricing Structure:

- Determine your pricing structure based on the value you provide, your expertise, and market rates. Consider offering different packages to accommodate various client needs and budgets.

Create a Professional Website:

- Establish an online presence through a professional website. Clearly communicate your consulting or coaching services, your background, and the value you bring. Include client testimonials, if available, to build credibility.

Promote Your Services on Your Podcast:

- Use your podcast as a platform to introduce your consulting or coaching services. Dedicate episodes to discussing the benefits of working with you, sharing success stories, and providing details on how interested listeners can sign up.

Utilize Social Media:

- Leverage social media platforms to promote your consulting/coaching services. Share snippets of your expertise, client testimonials, and any special promotions. Engage with your audience and encourage them to reach out for more information.

Create Marketing Materials:

- Develop professional marketing materials, including brochures, flyers, or digital assets, that highlight your consulting or coaching services.

Clearly articulate the value proposition and include a call-to-action for potential clients to contact you.

Offer Free Resources:

- Provide free resources on your website or through your podcast to showcase your expertise. This could include downloadable guides, webinars, or sample coaching sessions. This not only adds value to your audience but also acts as a marketing tool.

Implement a Booking System:

- Streamline the booking process by implementing an online scheduling system. This allows potential clients to easily book sessions with you, making the entire process efficient and user-friendly.

Deliver High-Quality Services:

- Once you have clients, prioritize delivering high-quality consulting or coaching services. Tailor your approach to each client's needs, provide actionable insights, and ensure a positive and impactful experience.

Gather Testimonials and Referrals:

- Collect testimonials from satisfied clients and encourage them to refer your services to others. Positive feedback and word-of-mouth recommendations can significantly contribute to the growth of your consulting or coaching business.

By following these steps, you can effectively transition your podcast expertise into a consulting or coaching business, providing valuable services to your audience while creating a new revenue stream for yourself.

Let's consider a fictional podcast named "Mindful Entrepreneur" hosted by Alex Turner, a business strategist and mindfulness advocate. Alex decides to offer consulting services to listeners who value his insights on combining business acumen with mindfulness practices. Here's an example of how he might structure his consulting services:

Podcast: *Mindful Entrepreneur*

Consulting Services Offered: Mindful Business Coaching

1. <u>Identify Your Expertise:</u>

   - *Alex Turner's podcast, "Mindful Entrepreneur," focuses on the intersection of mindfulness and business success. His expertise lies in guiding entrepreneurs to achieve professional growth while maintaining a balanced and mindful approach.*

2. <u>Understand Audience Needs:</u>

   - *Analyzing listener feedback, Alex notices a strong interest in applying mindfulness techniques to entrepreneurship. Listeners express a desire for personalized guidance in navigating challenges, fostering creativity, and achieving business goals.*

3. <u>Define Consulting Offerings:</u>

   - *Alex introduces "Mindful Business Coaching," offering*

one-on-one sessions to entrepreneurs seeking a mindful approach to business. Services include goal setting, stress management, decision-making strategies, and developing a mindful leadership style.

4. Set Pricing Structure:

- *Alex establishes a pricing structure that reflects the value of personalized coaching. He offers individual coaching sessions and package deals for ongoing support. The pricing is transparent and aligned with the transformational benefits clients can expect.*

5. Create a Professional Website:

- *Alex develops a professional website dedicated to his consulting services. The site showcases details about "Mindful Business Coaching," Alex's background, client testimonials, and an easy-to-use booking system for scheduling coaching sessions.*

6. Promote Services on the Podcast:

- *Alex dedicates podcast episodes to introduce his consulting services. He shares success stories, discusses the benefits of one-on-one coaching, and directs interested listeners to his website for more information and booking.*

7. Utilize Social Media:

- *Alex leverages social media platforms, particularly LinkedIn and Twitter, to promote his coaching services. He shares mindfulness tips for entrepreneurs, client success stories, and engages with his audience through polls and discussions on mindful business practices.*

8. Create Marketing Materials:

- *Alex develops visually appealing marketing materials, including a downloadable guide on "Mindful Leadership in Business" and brochures highlighting the benefits of his coaching services. These materials are shared on his website and social media platforms.*

9. Offer Free Resources:

- *As a teaser, Alex provides free resources such as a series of webinars on "Mindful Decision-Making for Entrepreneurs" and downloadable mindfulness exercises. These resources serve as an introduction to his expertise and encourage potential clients to explore his coaching services.*

10. Implement a Booking System:

- Alex integrates a user-friendly online booking system on his website, allowing entrepreneurs to easily view available coaching slots, choose suitable times, and book their sessions securely.

11. Deliver High-Quality Services:

- During one-on-one coaching sessions, Alex focuses on understanding each entrepreneur's specific challenges and goals. He provides tailored guidance, practical strategies, and ongoing support to help clients integrate mindfulness into their entrepreneurial journey.

12. Gather Testimonials and Referrals:

- Alex actively collects testimonials from entrepreneurs who have experienced positive transformations through his coaching services. Satisfied clients are encouraged to share their success stories and refer fellow entrepreneurs to benefit from mindful business coaching.

In this example, Alex Turner successfully extends his podcast expertise into personalized coaching services, offering valuable guidance to entrepreneurs seeking a mindful approach to business success.

CHAPTER 14

Incorporate Affiliate Codes to Earn a Commission

Using affiliate codes in your podcast promotions is an effective way to monetize your content. Here's a step-by-step guide on how to incorporate affiliate codes into your podcast:

Identify Relevant Affiliate Programs:
- Choose affiliate programs that align with your podcast content and resonate with your audience. Look for products or services that you genuinely believe in and that your listeners would find valuable.

Join Affiliate Programs:
- Sign up for the affiliate programs of the products or services you've identified. Most companies have an affiliate page on their website where you can apply to become an affiliate. Upon approval, you'll gain access to unique affiliate codes.

Understand Commission Structure:
- Familiarize yourself with the commission structure of each affiliate program. Understand how much commission you'll earn for each sale made through your affiliate link or code.

<u>Create Unique Affiliate Codes:</u>
- Some affiliate programs provide unique codes that your audience can use during checkout to attribute the sale to your podcast. If not, work with the affiliate program to generate custom codes that are easy for your listeners to remember.

<u>Integrate Codes into Podcast Content:</u>
- Seamlessly integrate affiliate codes into your podcast content. This can be done through dedicated ad spots, shout-outs, or product recommendations. Ensure that you provide clear instructions on how listeners can use the codes and the benefits they'll receive.

<u>Highlight Benefits for Listeners:</u>
- Emphasize the benefits or discounts that your listeners will receive by using your affiliate codes. This not only encourages them to make a purchase but also adds value to their experience.

<u>Track Performance:</u>
- Regularly monitor the performance of your affiliate codes. Most affiliate programs provide dashboards where you can track clicks, conversions, and commission earnings. Analyzing this data helps you understand which promotions are most effective.

<u>Diversify Affiliate Partnerships:</u>
- Explore partnerships with multiple affiliate programs to diversify your revenue streams. This can include collaborations with brands or

services that complement different aspects of your podcast content.

<u>Disclose Affiliate Relationships:</u>

- Maintain transparency with your audience by disclosing your affiliate relationships. Clearly communicate that you may earn a commission when they use your affiliate codes. This builds trust and ensures compliance with ethical guidelines.

<u>Create Engaging Content Around Affiliate Promotions:</u>

- Craft engaging content that integrates your affiliate promotions seamlessly. This could be in the form of storytelling, personal experiences, or in-depth reviews that resonate with your audience.

<u>Promote on Social Media and Other Platforms:</u>

- Extend your affiliate promotions beyond your podcast by promoting them on your social media channels, email newsletters, and other platforms. This widens your reach and increases the likelihood of conversions.

<u>Negotiate Exclusive Deals:</u>

- Work with affiliate partners to negotiate exclusive deals or discounts for your audience. Exclusive offers can be powerful incentives for your listeners to use your affiliate codes.

By following these steps, you can effectively incorporate affiliate codes into your podcast promotions, providing a monetization strategy that aligns with your content and benefits both you and your audience.

There are numerous affiliate programs across various industries, offering opportunities for content creators, bloggers, podcasters, and website owners to earn commissions by promoting products or services. Here are some examples of well-known affiliate programs:

Amazon Associates:

- Amazon's affiliate program allows participants to earn commissions on sales generated through their unique affiliate links. Affiliates can promote a wide range of products available on the Amazon platform.

ClickBank:

- ClickBank is a digital marketplace where affiliates can promote and earn commissions on a variety of digital products, including e-books, courses, and software.

ShareASale:

- ShareASale is an affiliate marketing network that connects affiliates with merchants offering a diverse range of products and services. Affiliates can choose from various merchants and promote their products.

Commission Junction (CJ Affiliate):

- CJ Affiliate is one of the largest affiliate marketing networks, providing access to a broad array of advertisers and products. Affiliates can find partnerships with well-known brands across different industries.

Rakuten Advertising:

- Rakuten, formerly known as Ebates, offers an affiliate program where affiliates can earn commissions by promoting products from partner retailers. It often features cash back incentives for shoppers.

ClickFunnels Affiliate Program:

- ClickFunnels is a platform for building sales funnels, and its affiliate program allows members to earn recurring commissions by promoting ClickFunnels subscriptions and related products.

Bluehost Affiliate Program:

- Bluehost, a web hosting provider, offers an affiliate program where affiliates can earn commissions for every customer who signs up for hosting services through their referral links.

Shopify Affiliate Program:

- Shopify's affiliate program allows individuals to earn commissions by promoting the popular e-commerce platform. Affiliates receive a commission for each customer who signs up for a paid Shopify plan.

HubSpot Affiliate Program:

- HubSpot's affiliate program enables affiliates to earn commissions by promoting HubSpot's CRM and marketing software. Affiliates can earn both one-time and recurring commissions.

Cratejoy Affiliate Program:

- Cratejoy is a subscription box marketplace, and its affiliate program allows participants to earn commissions by promoting various subscription box services available on the platform.

Semrush Affiliate Program:

- Semrush, a digital marketing tool, offers an affiliate program where individuals can earn recurring commissions by promoting Semrush subscriptions to marketers and SEO professionals.

Etsy Affiliate Program:

- Etsy's affiliate program allows affiliates to earn commissions by promoting unique handmade and vintage items available on the Etsy marketplace.

When participating in affiliate programs, it's important to review the terms and conditions, understand the commission structure, and choose programs that align with your audience and content niche. Always disclose your affiliate relationships to maintain transparency with your audience.

Let's create an example scenario for incorporating affiliate codes into a podcast. In this case, the podcast is called "Gourmet Delights" hosted by Alex, a food enthusiast. Alex decides to partner with a gourmet food affiliate program through CJ Affiliate, promoting a company called "ArtisanTaste."

Podcast: *Gourmet Delights*

Affiliate Partner: ArtisanTaste via CJ Affiliate

1. Identify Relevant Affiliate Program:

- *Alex identifies "ArtisanTaste," a high-end gourmet food company, as a relevant affiliate partner for the "Gourmet Delights" podcast. The company offers a variety of artisanal food products that align with the podcast's focus on culinary excellence.*

2. Join CJ Affiliate Program:

- *Alex joins the CJ Affiliate program, where ArtisanTaste is listed as one of the merchants. After a straightforward registration process, Alex gains access to unique affiliate codes and promotional materials.*

3. <u>Understand Commission Structure:</u>

- *CJ Affiliate provides a commission structure where affiliates earn a 12% commission on each sale generated through Alex's affiliate links for ArtisanTaste products. Alex reviews the terms to ensure a clear understanding of the commission structure.*

4. <u>Create Unique Affiliate Codes:</u>

- *Alex collaborates with ArtisanTaste to create a unique discount code for listeners of the "Gourmet Delights" podcast. The code "DELIGHT15" offers a 15% discount on any purchase and attributes the sale to the podcast.*

5. <u>Integrate Codes into Podcast Content:</u>

- *During episodes of "Gourmet Delights," Alex seamlessly integrates the affiliate code into the content. Alex talks about the exquisite flavors of ArtisanTaste products, shares personal experiences with the gourmet items, and encourages listeners to use the code for an exclusive discount.*

6. <u>Highlight Benefits for Listeners:</u>

- *Alex emphasizes that by using the affiliate code, listeners not only receive a discount on premium gourmet products but also support the "Gourmet Delights" podcast. Alex shares anecdotes about favorite ArtisanTaste products to add authenticity to the promotion.*

7. <u>Track Performance:</u>

- *Alex regularly monitors the performance of the affiliate code through the CJ Affiliate dashboard. The dashboard provides insights into clicks, conversions, and commission earnings associated with the podcast promotions.*

8. Diversify Affiliate Partnerships:

- *To offer a diverse range of gourmet options to listeners, Alex explores additional affiliate partnerships within the CJ Affiliate network. This might include collaborations with other artisanal food brands or kitchenware companies.*

9. Disclose Affiliate Relationships:

- *Alex maintains transparency by disclosing the affiliate relationship with ArtisanTaste in each episode. A brief disclaimer assures listeners that the podcast only promotes products and brands that align with its commitment to quality.*

10. Create Engaging Content Around Affiliate Promotions:

- Alex creates engaging content around ArtisanTaste promotions, such as featuring "Gourmet Delights Tasting Sessions" or interviewing chefs who endorse the brand. This content naturally integrates the affiliate code and provides valuable information to the audience.

11. Promote on Social Media and Other Platforms:

- Alex extends promotions to social media platforms, sharing visually appealing posts on Instagram and Pinterest. Alex encourages followers to use the affiliate code when indulging in gourmet experiences.

12. Negotiate Exclusive Deals:

- Alex negotiates with ArtisanTaste to provide exclusive deals during

special occasions or seasonal promotions. Exclusive offers, such as "Gourmet Holiday Gift Sets with Free Shipping," create a sense of exclusivity and entice listeners to make purchases.

In this example, Alex successfully incorporates the affiliate code from ArtisanTaste via CJ Affiliate into the "Gourmet Delights" podcast promotions, providing listeners with an exclusive discount while earning commissions for each sale generated through the affiliate links.

CHAPTER 15

Collaborate with Other Podcasters for Sponsorship or Joint Venture

Collaborating with other podcasters can be a fantastic way to expand your audience, share insights, and even explore revenue-generating opportunities. Here's a step-by-step guide on how to collaborate with other podcasters:

Identify Potential Podcast Partners:
- Look for podcasts that share a similar target audience or have complementary content. Consider podcasts that align with your niche or industry but may not be direct competitors.

Research and Listen to Their Content:
- Take the time to listen to episodes of the podcasts you're interested in collaborating with. Understand their style, content, and the preferences of their audience. This will help you tailor your collaboration proposal to align with their brand.

Establish Clear Objectives:
- Determine what you want to achieve through collaboration. Whether it's expanding your

audience, increasing brand awareness, or exploring revenue opportunities, having clear objectives will guide your collaboration efforts.

Reach Out with a Personalized Pitch:

- Craft a personalized pitch when reaching out to potential podcast partners. Clearly articulate the benefits of collaboration for both parties. Mention specific reasons why you believe your collaboration would be valuable for their audience.

Propose Joint Ventures:

- Joint ventures can include co-hosting special episodes, creating a series together, or collaborating on a unique project. Propose ideas that are mutually beneficial and align with the interests of both podcast audiences.

Explore Sponsorship Opportunities:

- Discuss potential sponsorship opportunities where you can cross-promote each other's podcasts. This could involve mentioning the partner's podcast in episodes or promoting specific episodes through social media and newsletters.

Cross-Promote Each Other's Episodes:

- Agree to cross-promote each other's episodes within your respective podcasts. This can be done through shout-outs, sharing snippets, or creating promo segments that are included in each other's episodes.

Coordinate Social Media Campaigns:

- Collaborate on social media campaigns to promote your joint venture or cross-promotions. Use hashtags, share behind-the-scenes content, and encourage your audiences to engage with both podcasts.

Host Joint Giveaways or Contests:

- Boost engagement by hosting joint giveaways or contests. This can involve promoting the same giveaway on both podcasts, encouraging listeners to follow both shows and engage with your content.

Consider Live Events or Webinars:

- Explore the possibility of hosting live events or webinars together. This could be a Q&A session, a panel discussion, or a workshop that brings value to both podcast audiences.

Negotiate Revenue-Sharing Models:

- If exploring revenue opportunities, discuss and negotiate revenue-sharing models. This could involve jointly promoting a sponsored product or service and sharing the proceeds.

Track and Analyze Results:

- Regularly track the results of your collaborations. Use podcast analytics, social media insights, and other metrics to understand the impact on your audience growth, engagement, and potential revenue.

Express Gratitude and Foster Long-Term Relationships:

- After the collaboration, express gratitude to your podcast partner. Consider ways to foster a long-term relationship, as recurring collaborations can bring sustained benefits to both parties.

Remember, successful collaboration is built on mutual respect, shared goals, and a genuine desire to provide value to your respective audiences. Approach collaborations with authenticity and creativity to make the most of these partnerships.

Let's create an example scenario where two podcasts, "Tech Trends Today" and "Digital Marketing Insights," collaborate on a joint venture to create a special series exploring the intersection of technology and digital marketing.

Podcast Collaboration Example: *"Tech Trends Today" & "Digital Marketing Insights"*

<u>Objective:</u>

- *To create a collaborative podcast series that delves into the latest technological trends impacting digital marketing strategies, providing valuable insights to both podcasts' audiences and potentially attracting joint sponsorships.*

<u>Steps Taken:</u>

Identify Potential Partners:
- *The hosts of "Tech Trends Today" and "Digital Marketing Insights" identified each other as potential*

collaboration partners due to the complementary nature of their content.

Research and Listen to Each Other's Content:

- *Both podcast hosts took the time to listen to several episodes of each other's podcasts to understand their style, audience, and content approach.*

Establish Clear Objectives:

- *The hosts discussed their objectives for collaboration, aiming to provide unique and valuable content to their audiences, increase cross-listener engagement, and explore potential joint sponsorships.*

Reach Out with a Personalized Pitch:

- *The host of "Tech Trends Today" reached out to the host of "Digital Marketing Insights" with a personalized pitch. The pitch highlighted the shared interests in technology and digital marketing and proposed a collaborative series that would benefit both podcast audiences.*

Joint Venture Proposal:

- *The proposal outlined a joint venture series titled "Tech & Marketing Convergence: Navigating the Digital Landscape." Each episode would explore a specific tech trend impacting digital marketing, with insights, case studies, and expert interviews.*

Sponsorship Opportunities:

- *Both hosts discussed potential sponsorship opportunities for the joint series. They identified a tech-related sponsor interested in reaching a combined audience interested in both technology and digital marketing.*

Cross-Promotion Strategy:

- *The hosts decided on a cross-promotion strategy where each podcast would feature promotional segments for the collaborative series. They agreed to include teaser clips, call-to-action messages, and shared social media posts leading up to the series launch.*

Live Launch Event:

- *To generate excitement, the hosts organized a live launch event on social media, where they introduced the collaborative series, answered audience questions, and provided exclusive behind-the-scenes content.*

Shared Social Media Campaigns:

- *Both hosts coordinated social media campaigns using a dedicated hashtag for the collaborative series. They encouraged their followers to engage with the content, share their thoughts, and participate in discussions.*

Joint Giveaway:

- *As part of the collaboration, the hosts organized a joint giveaway featuring tech gadgets and digital marketing tools. Listeners were encouraged to participate by subscribing to both podcasts and sharing their favorite episodes.*

Sponsorship Revenue Sharing:

- *The hosts negotiated a revenue-sharing model with the sponsor, where the proceeds from the joint sponsorship were distributed based on the number of impressions and engagements generated by each podcast.*

Track and Analyze Results:

- *Throughout the collaborative series, both hosts tracked metrics such as episode downloads, listener engagement, social media interactions, and the effectiveness of the joint sponsorship in generating revenue.*

Express Gratitude and Plan Future Collaborations:

- *After the successful collaboration, the hosts expressed gratitude to each other and the sponsor. They discussed the positive outcomes, lessons learned, and expressed interest in planning future collaborations to continue delivering valuable content to their audiences.*

In this example, the collaboration between "Tech Trends Today" and "Digital Marketing Insights" not only provided valuable insights to their audiences but also created a revenue-generating opportunity through joint sponsorships. This collaborative series showcased the potential for mutually beneficial partnerships in the podcasting space.

As you navigate the ever-evolving landscape of podcasting, we encourage you to continue your journey with passion, dedication, and a commitment to maximizing your profit potential. Here's a final message to inspire and guide you on your podcasting endeavors:

Stay Authentic:

- *Your authenticity is your greatest asset. Stay true to your voice, your style, and the unique perspective that sets your podcast apart. Authenticity builds trust with your audience, fostering long-term relationships that can translate into sustained profitability.*

Diversify Your Revenue Streams:

- *Explore diverse avenues for monetization. Whether it's through sponsorships, affiliate marketing, online courses, or collaborations, diversifying your revenue streams can create a resilient and stable income for your podcast.*

Leverage Collaborations:

- *Collaborate with fellow podcasters, industry experts, and potential sponsors. Joint ventures, cross-promotions, and collaborations can not only expand your audience but also open up new revenue opportunities. Strength lies in unity within the podcasting community.*

Optimize for Engagement:

- *Focus on creating engaging and valuable content. Your listeners are your biggest advocates. By optimizing for engagement, you not only retain your current audience but also attract new listeners, making your podcast an attractive platform for advertisers and sponsors.*

Harness the Power of Community:

- *Build a community around your podcast. Engage with your audience through social media, forums, and live events. A strong community not only enhances the overall podcast experience but also provides potential for crowdfunding, memberships, and exclusive content monetization.*

Adapt to Emerging Trends:

- *The podcasting landscape is dynamic. Stay informed about emerging trends, new technologies, and changes in listener behavior. By adapting to these shifts, you position yourself to leverage new opportunities and stay ahead in the evolving podcast ecosystem.*

Invest in Quality:

- *Invest in the quality of your content, production, and marketing. High-quality podcasts attract discerning listeners and are more appealing to potential sponsors. Remember, quality is a long-term investment that pays dividends in credibility and profitability.*

Optimize Monetization Strategies:

- *Continuously optimize your monetization strategies. Test different approaches, analyze performance metrics, and refine your methods. This iterative process ensures that you are maximizing your profit potential and staying attuned to what works best for your podcast.*

Celebrate Milestones:

- *Celebrate the milestones, both big and small. Whether it's reaching a subscriber milestone, securing a significant sponsorship, or launching a successful collaboration, take the time to acknowledge and celebrate your* achievements. It fuels your passion and motivates you to aim higher.

Embrace the Journey:

- Remember that the podcasting journey is a marathon, not a sprint. Embrace the process, learn from experiences, and enjoy the evolution of your podcast. By staying committed to your vision, you'll find fulfillment in both the creative process and the financial rewards.

Podcasters, your dedication to crafting compelling content has the power to captivate, inspire, and generate meaningful revenue. Keep pushing boundaries, exploring innovative strategies, and most importantly, have fun along the way.

Happy podcasting!

Jo Arcaya

ABOUT THE AUTHOR

Experienced Visionary, analyst and strategist in both business and politics. Handled award winning broadcast programs in business and news for 5 consecutive years as research specialists and writer in one of the largest broadcasting companies in the Philippines. His past experience in broadcasting is what influenced him in creating his own podcast "Feel Good with Jo Arcaya " a tagalog podcast catering Filipinoes around the world. It's available in all favorite podcast aps.

Entrepreneurship instructor at Golden Treasure Skills and Development Program Philippines. Experienced working in the consumer services industry. Skilled in Negotiation, Team Building, Strategic Planning, Social Media, and certified in Online Marketing. Contributes in mentoring as coach in Business & Development Network business plan competition. Graduated from Unibersidad De Manila (University of Manila) in fields of Political Science major in International Government. Experienced in managing few companies in Canada in integrated pest management, vegetation management, industrial, landscape, wildlife and structural which acquired certification during the transition of immigration to Canada.

Started regaining the previous skills in media production by producing Filipino World Channel (filipinoworldchannel.com) during the pandemic and grabbing the opportunity of the hike of the online media. Produced Canadian Experience Channel to help immigrants pass the Canadian Citizenship test.

Certified in music business from Berklee. Established a family business in music lesson, music composition, the Music Learning Center which you can check the website at https://www.musiclearning.ca.

If you want to collaborate with the author's podcast you may contact him at info@musiclearning.ca or josepharcaya@gmail.com.